I Remember Cape Cod

I Remember
CAPE COD

E. C. JANES

Drawings by Robert MacLean

THE STEPHEN GREENE PRESS
BRATTLEBORO, VERMONT

This book has been produced
in the United States of America:
designed by R. L. Dothard Associates,
composed, printed, and bound by The Colonial Press.
It is published by the Stephen Greene Press,
Brattleboro, Vermont 05301.

Library of Congress Cataloging in Publication Data
Janes, Edward C
    I remember Cape Cod.
    1. Janes, Edward C. 2. Cape Cod—Social life and
customs. I. Title.
PS3560.A47Z525   917.44'92'0340924 [B]   73-86032
ISBN 0-8289-0201-1

74 75 76 77 78 79 9 8 7 6 5 4 3 2 1

To Doris,

who didn't marry the Andover boy

Contents

A Horse
Counts Two

JOURNEYING by automobile through Massachusetts from
Westfield to Cape Cod, in the teen years of the century
was, like matrimony, a step not to be entered into lightly.
Two hundred miles of hill and also dale separated the two
locations, a vast expanse of *terra incognita* with strange place
names such as Upton, Bellingham, Wrentham and a distant
city known as Taunton. The successful accomplishment of
such a trip required considerable planning and careful
preparation. To paraphrase the Cunard slogan—getting
there may not have been half the fun but it was, at least, an
adventure of sorts.

It began with loading the 1913 Pope-Hartford touring
car by the dawn's early light of a summer morning. Earlier,
two wardrobe trunks filled with sheets, pillowcases, towels,
bathing suits, dresses, shirts and unmentionables had traveled Capeward by Railway Express, but considerable
impedimenta remained to be transported, along with five
humans, via Pope-Hartford.

The five included Father and Mother, my sister Doris,
Cousin Alfred and me. Cousin Alfred, a skinny, freckle-
faced youngster, was Aunt Lizzie's son, and he came along
with us each summer so that I would have a companion near
my age, although he was four years older. Our companion-
ship consisted fifty per cent of sharing our possessions and
fifty per cent of defending them from one another.
Occasionally, I wished him home in Chicopee where he
resided, but most of the time we were bosom companions. I

admired his somewhat swashbuckling demeanor and respected his greater knowledge of the world, even though I frequently became the victim of both these assets.

My sister Doris, a darkly pretty teen-ager, was an awesome personage to be humbly worshipped. Her knowledge of the world exceeded even Cousin Alfred's and her orbit touched rarified heights beyond my ken. Nevertheless, we were very close and she frequently served as a buffer from the world—and especially from Cousin Alfred—in times of stress.

In the matter of impedimenta, there was a steamer trunk, swaddled in oilcloth, to be strapped to the folding luggage carrier astern with suitcases tied on top. There was a five-gallon can of gasoline to be stowed between the two spare tires and the metal battery box on the left running board, for only the larger towns boasted garages where gasoline could be purchased from two-wheel Bowser carts. There was a complete medical kit to be placed on the floor of the front seat—Father was a doctor. There was a picnic lunch and there were various assorted cardboard boxes, paper bags and items of fishing tackle to be stuffed into available nooks and crannies.

With these preparations completed, it was time to garb ourselves for the road. For Mother and my sister Doris this consisted of donning linen dusters, gloves and veils. Father, Cousin Alfred and I wore dusters, caps and goggles with the addition, for Father, of heavy leather gauntlets.

Take-off time was usually set for 5:00 A.M., but what with last minute visits to the toilet—which led Father to inquire moodily why in hell the children couldn't go to the bathroom before getting into the car—forgetting to pack the fried chicken or to leave a note for the milkman, it was invariably nearer 5:30. But at last the great moment, long awaited and almost unbearably exciting, arrived. Dustered, capped, gloved and goggled, Father took his place behind the wheel and cried jovially, "We're off!" Frequently that was the last pleasant remark to be made for some time.

The Pope-Hartford, besides having a weldless steel front axle and roller bearings throughout, was equipped with a Grey and Davis self-starter, so-called, which was an innovation of the day and the last word in modern technology. When a round pedal beside the clutch was depressed, the starter said, "Ahroo-ah! Ahroo-ah! Ahroo-ah!" in loud and confident tones. Sometimes it said, "Ahroo-ah!" quite a few times before anything happened, which led Mother to inquire testily why in Heaven's name the engine couldn't be warmed up ahead of time before we were all in the car. To which Father replied stiffly that he had set the spark plugs and had filled the grease cups that morning and that obviously the car must have started earlier or it would still have been in the barn and not here beside the carriage step.

Sometimes Father had to unpack the crank from under the front seat and toilsomely revolve the flywheel by hand. But usually, after a shorter or longer time, the engine would cough and then snort into glorious thirty-horsepower life.

We were all very proud of that Grey and Davis starter in 1913. Leaving from inns, stores or other gathering places, we smiled patronizingly as we watched less fortunate drivers manually cranking their engines. But by 1918—people didn't trade cars every year or two in those days—it was another story. By then Detroit expertise had superseded the Grey and Davis with more efficient, quieter starters and we were forced to sit red-faced and with averted eyes while loud *ahroo-ahs* shattered the silence, causing heads to turn in wonder.

Sometimes, when the engine was still hot after a brief stop, merely turning on the ignition switch would cause the engine to catch. What quieter starter than that! Then one could beam condescendingly again and one could stick out one's tongue at the fat youth lolling on the seat of the 1918 Locomobile.

As we rolled out of Westfield, Father accelerated to twenty-two miles an hour. This was known as the "chauffeur's speed" and theoretically enabled one to average twenty miles an hour. It was too optimistic an hypothesis, but, as Father said, "If you keep her on twenty-two all day, you wouldn't want to walk back home at night." Actually, treadless tires, rutted paved roads and washboardy, dusty or muddy dirt roads made twenty-two miles an hour an unattainable speed except under optimum conditions.

The first real test of the Cape-bound trip came five miles outside of Westfield on the road to Springfield. Here, Tatham Hill upreared its fearsome 30 per cent grade and, to make matters worse, you couldn't get a good start before reaching it because of the sharp curve over the railroad bridge.

Father did his best, though. Leaning slightly forward and clutching the wheel firmly in both hands, he pushed the accelerator to the floor, charging full tilt at the hill. At the same time he played his ace-in-the-hole. There was another round pedal located just below the driver's seat, and if you jammed it down hard with your heel, as Father did now, it shut off the muffler. The resulting splendid uproar was like that of a jet fighter taking off, and it gave one almost the same sense of magnificent power. To leave his right foot free for this operation, Father shifted from the accelerator to the hand throttle on the steering wheel. For good measure he advanced the spark lever beside it.

Quivering, the speedometer needle rose to 30 . . . 35 . . . 40 miles per hour! Like a rocket, we zoomed past a clanging trolley car and attacked the hill head-on. Sheer momentum carried us halfway up the grade; it was the second half that posed the test. Slowly, the speedometer needle dropped—35 . . . 30 . . . 25. At 15 Father resorted to second gear. By now the trolley had come up with us and was pulling ahead, but by a quick manipulation of the spark lever, Father made it a dead heat. As we breasted the hill, Father released the muffler cut-out pedal and in the ensuing comparative silence summed up the triumph just accomplished.

"Quite a car," he said, giving the wheel an affectionate pat. "Not many will take Tatham Hill like that."

Three hours and twenty minutes later we were rolling along Main Street in Worcester, sixty long miles from home. Thus far our way had lain through more or less familiar country, but now it was time to strike out into the unknown. As an aid to navigation, Father carried a set of blue cards furnished by the Automobile Legal Association. These were primitive ancestors of the modern road books, and a comparison of them with today's guides might be likened to a comparison between Columbus's magnetized needle in a straw floating in a bowl of water and a present-day marine compass. To use them it was necessary to set the odometer at zero.

Reading the cards to Father as he drove was accounted a great honor and gave one a sense of playing a major role in the success of the expedition. At least it did to my sister and Cousin Alfred. I couldn't read at the time and so was unable to participate in the project, but they fought bitterly and vociferously for the coveted post. Finally, Mother would settle the argument by decreeing that, as a young lady, Doris would have the first turn of a half-hour's duration and then Alfred would take over for a similar period.

Thereupon my sister, Doris, filled with a sense of importance, would take up her duties, her voice somewhat muffled by her veil. "Mileage zero. Follow Main Street to Grafton Street and turn right with trolley tracks. . . ."

The creators of these cards seem to have been filled with a sense of the permanence of earthly things, a faith that frequently proved completely unjustified.

"Eight and three-tenths miles. Turn left at intersection past large oak tree," the cards and my sister advised, and lo, there was no oak tree. Or "Twelve and one-tenth miles. Bear left past red barn on right," where only a gaping cellar hole remained.

But from practice, you learned to interpret the cards' intent, even when they bade you: "Turn right and keep right on Front Street." And if, as occasionally happened, you did become lost, you could always eventually find someone from whom to ask directions . . . as Father did from the grizzled farmer carting home a load of feed.

"Can you tell me the way to Franklin?" Father inquired.

"Yep," the farmer replied.

There followed a long pause, after which Father pressed on. "Well, is this the right road?"

"Yep," the farmer said and then, as Father released the brake, added amiably, "But you're goin' the wrong way on it."

When his turn came, Cousin Alfred's interpretation of the cards sometimes furthered their obscurity through his inability to pronounce some of the words. As when he solemnly intoned, "Forty and four-tenths miles. Bear left to ass-end hill." But at nine you can't be expected to know all the words.

Eventually, watching fields and woods, villages and cities drift by—and even reading the magic route cards—began to pall, and it was time to seek recreation in other diversions. Besides quarreling, there were several. While Mother took over the ALA route cards, the rest of us plunged into a rousing game of roadside cribbage.

Proceeding at twenty-two miles an hour through a countryside well populated by horses, cows, dogs, cats, sheep and even goats—to say nothing of rabbits and squirrels—roadside cribbage reached an apogee in pre–World War I years that it could not possibly sustain in these days of speeding cars, superhighways and suburban sprawl.

Under a scoring system in which a cow counted one, a horse two, a dog five, a cat ten, sheep and goats twenty-five and wild animals thirty-five, it usually didn't take long to reach one hundred points or game. The difficulty was in trying to keep an accurate count of large herds of cows scattered over hillside pastures and to glimpse flocks of sheep almost hidden by wooded slopes.

Since action was divided between the left and right sides of the road, we chose teams. Everyone tried to enlist Mother as a teammate, for she had eagle eyes that could locate a horse grazing at the edge of a woodlot on a distant hill or a squirrel sitting in the crotch of a roadside tree.

Her eyesight was surpassed only by that of Cousin Alfred, who descried thirty cows in a herd of ten and saw cats and dogs invisible to everyone else. One day he claimed to have seen an elephant; to teach him the sorry wages of mendacity, Father backed the car and, sure enough, in a stream below a covered bridge stood a pachyderm attended by a man in a red uniform, a member of an itinerant carnival.

The game of roadside cribbage invariably ended in a battle. When peace was restored, we turned our attention to another pastime known as automobile poker. The object of this game was to make up poker hands from the license plates of cars coming toward us. At the leisurely pace at which two vehicles approached one another in those days, one had ample time to work out the best combination of figures. Also, few cars in that era had more than five digits on their plates.

Having decided who should take the first car, second and third turns were divided among the other two players and from there on we played in rotation. The only trouble was that cars were often spaced so far apart that a single "hand" might go on for many suspenseful minutes. You could, of course, make two pairs out of a plate with the numbers 32243 or a full house out of 56565.

It was thus early, as a by-product of motor trips to Cape Cod, that I learned that three of a kind beats two pair and a straight beats three of a kind, information that was to serve me well in later years. The knowledge was dearly bought, for Cousin Alfred, unbeknownst to my parents, proposed that we play for money, and sometimes my twenty-five cents a week allowance remained in hock to him for the first two weeks of our vacation.

Automobile poker, like roadside cribbage, ended when the participants were about to come to blows. By then, though, it was usually time for lunch, a feature us younger tourists had been loudly requesting ever since leaving Springfield. There were no roadside rest areas, complete with tables, fireplaces and waste receptacles in this simpler era; would-be picnickers were strictly on their own.

The annual ritual began with Mother's announcement, "It's nearly noon, George. When we see a nice place, we'd better stop and have our picnic."

"Very well," Father would concur, unconsciously accelerating to twenty-five miles an hour.

Fifteen minutes and five miles later, Mother would remark, "There's a pretty spot by that brook, George."

"Sorry. Didn't see it," Father would reply, pressing on. "There'll be another."

There was, but Father didn't see that one, either. Eventually, though, he would pull to the side of the road. "How's this?" he would inquire genially.

My sister's "Oh, Daddy!" would mingle with Mother's "Oh, George!"

"What's wrong with this?" Father would demand, looking hurt.

Mother explained. "It's right out in the broiling sun with nothing to look at but that rundown farm and it smells of cow."

"All right. You pick a place."

"I've been trying," Mother noted. "We've passed several lovely spots, but you've been going so fast you couldn't stop. Drive slowly now, and see if we can find a good place."

Along about one o'clock, famished and with tempers frayed, we would come to a halt at a compromise spot. While the Ladies' Auxiliary made ready the picnic, Father, Cousin Alfred and I strolled nonchalantly cross-country to disappear among the bushes. Service stations with rest rooms had not yet been heard of, and as a result, feminine travelers, especially, often found themselves in an unenviable position. Father allowed brief comfort stops at the Bancroft Hotel in Worcester and the Taunton railroad station, but, aside from these concessions, self-discipline was the watchword for the ladies.

By the time Father, Cousin Alfred and I returned from our relief expedition, Mother had superintended the spreading of our automobile robe upon the ground and the placing thereon of plates of fried chicken, bread and butter sandwiches, potato chips, hardboiled eggs, pickles, celery, olives, tomatoes, cookies and fruit. Thermos bottles, one of lemonade for the children and one of iced tea for the adults, perched precariously on the sidelines, and around this festive robe we arranged ourselves, paper plates in hand, for a half-hour of solid enjoyment.

When we had finished eating, Father lighted a relaxing cigar while Mother packed up any remaining food—"We can have this for snacks later"—and placed the trash in a separate container. Cousin Alfred and I explored the neighboring woods; Doris, who was in love, sat cross-legged on the ground trying to look inscrutable.

A blast on the Pope-Hartford's klaxon brought Alfred and me, sweaty and panting from the woods, to find Father

making final preparations to resume our journey. He had removed the cushion from the front seat and unscrewed the cap of the gasoline tank located beneath it. Now he produced a funnel with a piece of chamois tucked into it. From the can on the running board, he poured gasoline through the chamois filter until his wooden stick gauge showed the tank to be half full.

"That ought to take us to Taunton," he asserted. "All right. All aboard."

And so we were off again, refreshed. "One hundred ten miles and four-tenths. Turn right at intersection onto North Road, which follow to Bellingham. . . ."

Somewhere between Westfield and Cape Cod there was

sure to be at least one puncture and sometimes more. Our record on one memorable trip was six. The Pope-Hartford carried an optimistic two spare tires in canvas cases strapped to the running board. If these did not suffice, you had to resort to the patching kit. Blowouts, of course, were something else.

Secretly, I welcomed the occasional puncture. Being too young to help change tires, I looked forward to these unscheduled interruptions of the trip because they gave Cousin Alfred and me opportunities to stretch our legs in races up and down the road or in looking for snakes in adjacent fields. But Father was not of a like mind. And one could scarcely blame him, for changing tires in those days was a dirty, sweaty and sometimes painful operation.

The first obstacle with which one had to contend was the folding jack, whose propensity to fold increased in direct ratio to the wheel's height from the ground. Usually, along about the fourth try, Father succeeded in raising the car to a point where the offending tire could be removed. There it poised in delicate balance while Father attacked the bolts that held the rim to the wheel.

If Cousin Alfred and I didn't enter into our road-running or snake-hunting activities voluntarily, we were firmly bidden by Mother to absent ourselves from the immediate vicinity of the stranded car. Then Mother and Doris went to gather wildflowers in neighboring meadows, leaving Father free to exercise the considerable vocabulary that he had built up in former similar emergencies and that aided him immeasurably in their resolution.

Sometimes when Father took off the punctured tire or tried to put on the spare, the jack suddenly folded, but if he was fortunate, it held until the bolts were replaced and the offending flat tire kicked and placed on the running board. Then a surly snarl of the klaxon would summon us from field and roadside and Father would rub grimy hands and grease-smooched face with a towel before taking his place behind the wheel once more. According to the rules, wildflowers could be carried on to our destination, but snakes or frogs, if any, had to be left behind or else surreptitiously held captive in one's pocket until they could be more safely and securely housed.

Almost as bad as a puncture was putting up the top of our vehicle when, as frequently happened, a sudden shower or thunderstorm swept down upon us. If a steady rain was falling at the time of departure, the top could be raised at leisure in the dry comfort of the garage. But when summer thunderstorms caught us on the road, we were sitting ducks.

"It looks black in the west, George," Mother would venture, glancing apprehensively at the sky.

"It'll go around us," Father invariably replied, and the wish was father to the thought.

When it became apparent that the storm would not go around but was bearing relentlessly down upon us, Father resignedly pulled to the side of the road and disembarked to do battle with the top.

The first step was to loosen the large bolts, one on each side, that held the top in place. They invariably stuck, and before they finally surrendered to the onslaught of a stout wrench, the first large drops were splashing down. At this point our group dug out rain gear from under boxes, bags and fishing tackle and struggled into it.

When the bolts had at last been loosened, one could then

remove the three steel bars to which the folded canvas was fastened and heave the top up and forward in a sort of sweeping motion. One could, that is, if one were possessed of superhuman strength and agility. Atlas undoubtedly could have done it and it would probably have given Hercules scant trouble, but to mere mortals it proved an insurmountable obstacle. Two able-bodied men might have been able to conquer that top. But Father was alone.

Father tried all manner of stratagems, attempting to catch the top unawares or to wrestle it into position by brute force. He even tried standing on the hood, but the top withstood his best efforts. And by now the rain was descending in torrents, flooding boxes, bags and suitcases and soaking the humans huddled in the tonneau.

"Please hurry, George," Mother would suggest. "We're getting drowned."

About then, working on the theory that two boys are equal to one man, Cousin Alfred and I were pressed into service to haul on one side while Father hauled on the other.

"Now!" Father exhorted grimly.

And, grunting and straining, the three of us fought the top into place. But the job wasn't finished yet. First, Father had to place the lugs in the steel bars into the proper holes at the sides of the car. And when he let go of his side of the top, it tried to fold back to its original closed position again. But while I held one side, Cousin Alfred ran around to take Father's place while Father inserted the lugs into the holes and fastened them.

Now the top assumed the droopy appearance of a pup tent pitched by a tenderfoot Boy Scout, but at least only Father, Cousin Alfred and I were getting wet. To complete the top raising, it was necessary to fasten two long leather straps, one on each side, from the front of the top to rings fastened for the purpose to the fenders. Then it was only the work of another ten minutes to fit and button the side curtains in place. Often by then the storm had ended and the sun was beginning to peep through the clouds.

These were the ordinary vicissitudes that beset the motorist. There were others, less common, such as a steaming radiator—Father carried a collapsible canvas bucket to overcome that hazard—or becoming mired in hub-deep mud or sand. But even this problem was not insoluble, for you could usually find a farmer with a team of stout horses or oxen, ready to pull you out for whatever fee he thought the traffic would bear. If motor trouble developed, repairs were usually not too complicated, especially since Father carried practically another Pope-Hartford with us in spare parts.

About this time it began to seem as though Cape Cod were some nebulous Promised Land, remote and unattainable. It seemed that we would go on and on forever, past fields and woods and farms and through villages—"Turn left past blacksmith shop and proceed around numerous curves to Lake Pearl. . . ."

And then, magically, ahead appeared the first cranberry bog! At the sight, weariness and lethargy vanished, to be replaced by a fever of anticipation, nostrils aquiver for the first breath of salt air, eyes straining for the first glimpse of salt water. That came at Buzzard's Bay where we rolled across one of the drawbridges of the newly completed Cape Cod Canal.

Once across the Canal, the Promised Land had been

main Street, Wellfleet

gained. The remaining sixty miles to Wellfleet were sheer delight compounded of scrub oak and pine woods, dunes, cranberries, beach plums, bayberries, shimmering ponds, sleepy villages, spreading elms, two-wheeled carts and wide, blue vistas of ocean and bay.

What matter now if a puncture or two intervened between us and our destination? We were on the Cape and we sat forward eagerly watching for familiar landmarks to come into view . . . the tower on Scargo Hill in Dennis, the Marconi wireless masts at South Wellfleet. And at last we rolled through the main street of Wellfleet and turned into the oyster-shell road that led to our cottage.

Numbed limbs and weariness were forgotten as we rushed into the beloved house which seemed, somehow, to welcome us like an old friend. All looked the same as when we had left last Labor Day—the trunks lined up on the porch, the beds waiting to be made up, the cupboard doors open to receive their complement of groceries.

From room to room we roamed, to see that everything was still here and in its place, and to breathe in the wonderful aroma of a house just opened, mingled with salt air. From house to backyard to barn we raced in a whirlwind exploration. When it was done, we knew that all was well and that another Cape Cod summer had begun.

Home Away
from Home

ACCOMMODATIONS for vacationers on Cape Cod in the years before World War I consisted of cottages and hotels. Occasionally, one might see a tent pitched on a deserted beach or the shore of some lonely, wooded pond, but camping was considered eccentric behavior and those who practiced it were suspect. Tourist homes and motels were still far beyond the distant horizon.

"Cottages" varied all the way from glorified shacks bearing names such as Suitsus and Weadoreit up to the palatial estates of Chatham, Hyannisport and Craigville. Most placed somewhere in the middle. One thing practically all had in common—they were located in town and within walking distance of both stores and the beach.

Our family domicile was a modest white frame dwelling that the owner, whose birthplace it was, had turned into a two-family home. We rented the downstairs, and the Hopkins family, who owned the house, lived above us. In addition to Mr. and Mrs. Hopkins, the Hopkins family included two daughters, Emmy and Ruby, who were about my sister's age.

Our apartment consisted of a small entry hall that opened on the left into a large dining room—which we also used as a living room—and on the right into a large living room—which we also used as a bedroom; the master bedroom, in fact, where Mother and Father slept. Adjacent to that was the chamber I shared with Cousin Alfred. A

short hall led to Doris's bedroom; stairs from this hall led to the Hopkins apartment above.

At the rear of the dining room one entered a good-sized kitchen furnished with an iron sink, a wood range, a three-burner kerosene stove, an ice chest and a table. The bathroom, so to speak, was located some fifty feet behind the house in the woodshed adjoining the barn. This was convenient because, following the custom of the time, everyone who visited the facility by day or by night was expected to bring back two or three pieces of wood for the kitchen range.

At one time, when the house had been lived in year-round, a Franklin stove had heated the living room and you could still see where it had reposed in front of a metal-covered stovepipe hole in the wall beneath the mantel. But now the kitchen range supplied the only heat we had to take the chill from foggy August nights—that and the patchwork quilts with which each bed was furnished.

The house was situated on a high bluff overlooking the wide waters of Wellfleet Bay some half-mile away. On clear days you could trace the curving shore of the Cape past Eastham and Orleans to Brewster, Dennis and Barnstable across the blue bay. And at night, from the yard or the bedroom windows, you could see the steady gleam of nearby Mayo's Beach Light and the winking beam of Billingsgate Light flashing on the dark horizon.

For this menage Father paid the then considerable rent of forty dollars a month. At even twice this amount, however, we felt it would have been a bargain, for over the many summers that we stayed there, it became to us a second and well-beloved home.

In those years the Cape and Vineyard Electric Company had not yet stretched its wires along the Outer Cape and we depended upon kerosene lamps for light—small hand lamps to light us to bed, and large, ornate lamps in dining room and living room to illuminate our evening activities.

Two or three times a summer, Cousin Alfred and I were dispatched to Wiley's grocery store with a spouted can to fetch oil. Mr. Wiley hand-cranked the kerosene—which he called coal oil—from a large tank and then jammed a potato down over the spigot. We also used kerosene oil for cooking and a little for the Pope-Hartford as well, for though its headlights were electric, its sidelights and tail lights burned kerosene.

There was also a lamp post in front of the house. The post remained bare during the day, but toward dusk, a man named Monkey Baker used to come along, first behind a team and later in a truck, carrying a dozen or so lamps which he lighted and placed on the posts along Holbrook Avenue. These, however, illuminated the encircling darkness only feebly, and when one walked abroad at night, it was practically essential to carry a flashlight to keep one's path and avoid stepping upon the myriads of toads which thronged the streets on their nocturnal hunt for insects.

Since there was no electricity, there were no electric pumps, and water for drinking, washing and laundering had to be pumped by hand from a deep well behind the house. The long-handled red pump had a hook on its lip where you could hang a bucket, and when you had finished filling it, the excess water in the pump discharged into a large wooden tub which also provided a handy, if temporary, repository for frogs, turtles and minnows. The water, unchlorinated or otherwise treated, was cold as ice and about as hard.

Pumping a pitcher of water for the table was no chore,

but pumping tubs full of water for baths or for the weekly laundry was a different story and Cousin Alfred and I used many stratagems in attempts to foist this onerous task upon one another. At first we tried pleading illness or injury, but this soon became too transparent and we were forced to invent more elaborate wiles.

The best I could come up with was to hide in the dank earth cellar of the barn, from which I was shortly flushed by searching parties, but Cousin Alfred was made of more imaginative stuff. When pump duty called, he pretended a prior and more urgent call of nature and betook himself to the friendly shelter of the convenience in the woodshed. No one could well interfere with this necessary function, and there he would sit reading smuggled copies of the *Police Gazette* until I had filled the tubs.

The furnishings of our summer home were a somewhat bizarre combination of Victorian and neo–Sears Roebuck. The brass or painted oak beds and the curved-top dressers, the assortment of mission, leather-flounced and reed chairs, the Roman sofa and fancy-shaped tables were strictly Gay Nineties. So were the golden oak commodes, complete with pitcher, bowl and chamber pot. But the Wehrle six-hole range, the Miracle kerosene stove and the Economy ice chest in the kitchen, the decorated clam shell ashtrays and pink, bead-fringed Beauty Special lamps in the dining and living rooms, and the blue and green floral-design Axminister carpet on the living room floor were up-to-the-minute mod.

The ships came somewhere in between. These took the form of pictures, and they ranged in size from modest 18 x 20 inch prints to 3 x 4 foot paintings done on metal. These

latter masterpieces depicted ocean greyhounds of the time—
the sort of thing one sees in travel bureau offices. There
were a lot of them; assembled, they would have comprised
an imposing, if heterogeneous fleet.

In the dining room hung pictures of the S.S. *Rotterdam*,
the S.S. *Mauritania*, and the S.S. *Olympic*, all under full
steam. Seated in the living room, one could enjoy color
prints of the racing yacht *America*, the clipper ship
Dreadnaught off Tuskar Light, the clipper ship *Flying Cloud*
and the frigate *Constitution* rounding Elba and making
heavy weather of it. The bedroom I shared with Cousin
Alfred boasted portraits of the pilot boat *Wm. J. Romer* and
the clipper ship *Red Jacket*. In Doris's boudoir one could
inspect a lithograph showing the steamship *Great Eastern*
and a canvas of the *Entrance to Boston Harbor, 1881*. A
modest print of the schooner *Artemis* decorated the wall of
the front hall. As a bemused guest from the hinterlands
remarked after touring our menage, "My God, you can get
seasick here lying right in bed!"

Besides their aesthetic appeal, these pictures had a
practical application as well, serving as convenient hiding
places for contraband. For years Cousin Alfred kept his
packs of Sweet Caporal cigarettes behind the *Wm. J.
Romer*. Doris hid chocolate bars and love letters in back of
the *Great Eastern* and I had my own cache of cornsilk-and-
toilet-paper cigarettes stowed behind the clipper *Red Jacket*.

To Mr. Hopkins, these *objets d'art*, and others which he
kept upstairs, were as precious as a collection of Botticellis or
Picassos might be to other connoisseurs. Contemplating one
or another of his favorites, he would sigh with satisfaction
and observe, "I gorry, you can almost taste the salt water."

In his day, Mr. Hopkins had tasted a lot of it. At the time, he was employed as a salesman for a rubber concern in Springfield, Massachusetts, and could only join his family at the shore for his two-week vacation in August. But though land-bound now, in an earlier day he had followed the sea, first as cabin boy at the age of twelve on the schooner *Unis P. Newcomb* out of Wellfleet and later as able-bodied seaman and mate of a succession of schooners, barks and brigs until his mid-twenties. Then hard times along the coast turned him inland to seek a living.

Afloat or ashore, Mr. Hopkins ran a taut ship. The sea was in his blood, and one of its tenets impelled him to keep things shipshape and in apple-pie order. His arrival on the first of August was the signal for frenzied activity at the Hopkins homestead. He would arrive on the noon train from Boston dressed in a neat business suit and stiff-collared white shirt, only to emerge an hour later garbed like a character out of *Moby Dick*.

His costume seldom varied. It consisted of khaki trousers, a gray flannel shirt with a red bandana knotted at the throat, a tan canvas cap with a leather visor, and brown sneakers which he sometimes exchanged for rubber hip boots drooping about his knees.

Father affected a similar style, except that he wore a turned-down sailor hat. When they walked abroad together, it appeared that some coasting schooner or fishing smack had just put into port. One of the finest compliments Father ever received came one day when he and Mr. Hopkins were passing the depot on their way to net bait at the railroad trestle. The morning train had just discharged a sprinkling of city vacationers who were still standing on the platform as Father and Mr. Hopkins walked by. A newly arrived tourist touched his wife's arm.

"Look!" Father overheard him exclaim. "There are a couple of old salts now. You can tell them very time!"

Little more than an hour after his arrival, Mr. Hopkins would be embarked upon a strenuous program of refurbishment. From the cluttered interior of the barn came tubs of whitewash and cans of red paint to be applied with a lavish hand until not a drop remained. The first objects to be attacked were the stones.

At some earlier time, before our introduction to Cape Cod and Mr. Hopkins, he had brought back from Chequesset Neck, after what must have been back-breaking toil, a load of stones, each one about the size, as he put it, "of a codfish's head." These sizable rocks he had placed in a row about a foot apart to mark the boundary between his lot and that of the Morning Glory summer cottage next door. He had also encircled the flag pole and the trunk of the silver oak tree with stones, and had made a border around the flower bed in front of the house.

Each summer these stones received a fresh coat of whitewash and leftover whitewash was used to stripe the oak tree trunk. It was with the red paint, though, that Mr. Hopkins really let himself go. He spread it generously over the porch chairs and lawn furniture in the backyard, over the swing, the bird houses, and the stakes and rings made from sail hoops which we used to play ring toss.

Some years he added a dab of red paint to the tops of the whitewashed stones and sometimes he painted red stripes to alternate with the white ones on the oak tree. The effect was striking in the extreme and, as Mr. Hopkins himself remarked, it "gave the place an air."

The yard and the barn comprised Mr. Hopkins's domain and here, though his Cape-reared wife discouraged his artistic talents indoors, he could do as he wished. As a result, the barn became a monument to his ingenuity. Its wide front door, high enough to admit a load of marsh hay, gaped open throughout the summer in sunshine and in rain.

Scrap lumber, saw horses, broken furniture, cans of paint and turpentine, pails, clam rakes, fishing tackle, lanterns, garden tools, wagon wheels, boxes of nails and screws, empty kegs, fish nets, jugs, wooden decoys, pieces of old harness, a rusty musket, coils of rope, crocks, cork floats and old bottles crammed its dim interior, but Mr. Hopkins had cleared an area the size of a small room at the front of the building. Here a faded green carpet covered the floorboards.

In its center, on a square of battered linoleum, sat a brass cuspidor and conveniently around it reposed a half-circle of beat-up chairs, long since banished from the house. Dog-eared sporting scenes, clipped from old calendars, adorned a nearby wall and over all hung a pervasive smell of salt, tar, hemp, paint and tobacco which even the fiercest northeast gale could not dissipate. Indeed, a spell of rain and wind only seemed to intensify the aroma in all its subtle nuances. This was Mr. Hopkins' sanctum, the castle that sheltered him from the troublous world outside.

Ours was one type of summer home. Another, perhaps more typical, was rented by our friends, the Halls, from Wakefield, Massachusetts. Their large, rambling shingled house stood overlooking the bay on a high bluff from which a long flight of steps led directly to the beach. This cottage boasted a screened porch which extended across its entire front. Also a small fireplace in which the Halls burned driftwood picked up along the beach.

But if more elegant in these appointments, the Hall cottage lacked the furniture and furnishings that ours contained. No ships, no carpets, no elegant sofas, chairs or beds graced its rooms, not even a Wehrle range. Illumination came from kerosene lamps in wall brackets, and the bare wooden walls of the living room, dining room and four upstairs bedrooms were decorated, like Mr. Hopkins' barn, with prints from old calendars and a Charles Dana Gibson picture or two.

And their furniture consisted of reed chairs and sofa, deal tables and wooden beds. They cooked on a kerosene stove, pumped water as we did, and their "bathroom" was installed in a small edifice behind the house, naked and undisguised, unlike ours which hid away in the woodshed. Cottages such as this, interspersed with Wee Cottes and Dunroamins, sprinkled the shores of bay and ocean in villages from Bourne to Provincetown.

Summer hotels of the time were equally variegated. They included deluxe hostelries such as the Chatham Bars Inn and the Hotel Belmont in Harwich-by-the-Sea. They included a sprinkling of small, snug inns and a number of rambling, wooden edifices that ranked somewhere between the deluxe resorts and the inns. All operated on the American plan and all were distinguished by wide porches featuring a line of chairs in which guests rocked and digested the gargantuan meals served three times a day.

One of the popular medium-sized hotels of the time was the Chequesset Inn at Wellfleet, which advertised itself as

"The Hotel Over The Sea." It was owned, as was much of the surrounding real estate, by Captain Lorenzo Dow Baker, founder of the United Fruit Company and the first man to bring bananas to the United States.

Having become wealthy as a result of this venture, he proceeded to spend some of his money in developing his native homeland. His holdings included Great Island, Chequesset Neck, the land around several ponds, the steamship wharf at Provincetown and other properties on

The Chequessett Inn

the Outer Cape. He played a major role in the erection of the Pilgrim Monument at Provincetown. And he built the Chesquesset Inn.

The inn, which could accommodate upwards of a hundred guests, was located toward the western end of Mayo's Beach and was constructed on a wide pier extending several hundred feet into the bay. You could drive a car the length of the pier, past doors marked *Purser, Salon* and *Smoking Room*. Having spent much of his life at sea, Captain Baker patterned his hotel as nearly as possible after the United Fruit steamers which passed along the Back Shore of Cape Cod on their way to and from Jamaica and Central American ports.

The dining room and one or two other public rooms had large skylights and, to the Captain, the third story was the "boat deck." The interior was done in oak with massive beams and the second and third-story bedrooms were constructed to resemble a ship's cabins.

A catwalk led from the pier to a large float to which was tethered a flotilla of skiffs, and beyond the pier the naphtha launch *Osprey* rode proudly at anchor. Guests could row about the harbor in the skiffs or they could charter the *Osprey* and its morose-looking skipper to take them on deep-sea fishing expeditions or on picnics to Great Island and Billingsgate.

At the land end of the pier, a sort of annex housed the help, mostly youngsters recruited from New England colleges. A bowling alley, a stucco garage, a row of bathhouses and a tennis court were located across the road from the beach and behind them rose a bluff crowned by a water tower whose platform afforded a wide, paroramic view across the bay.

The Chequesset Inn boasted flush toilets and even electric lights. The electricity came from a gasoline-powered Delco system installed in the garage. Quite often, though, the system proved unequal to the load placed upon it, causing the lights to dim and blink. In order to conserve electricity, the lights were turned off at ten-thirty; this hour, according to the management, was high time for folks to be in bed, anyway. Those who insisted on prolonging their nocturnal revels were forced to conduct them within the cramped confines of the bathrooms, where feeble night lights glimmered until dawn.

A leaflet the Inn mailed to prospective guests listed in the way of entertainment "Sea and Lake Fishing, Boating, Bathing, Tennis, Billiards, Bowling, Orchestra." All these activities were indeed available and furnished diversion for young and old. What the leaflet failed to mention were the spirited late-evening poker games (which took place in the bathrooms) and the entertainments in the salon.

We are apt to think of today as a do-it-yourself era. Guests of the Chequesset Inn were doing-it-themselves a half-century ago. True, there was a trio—today we would call it a combo—which furnished music for sipping tea, for eating dinner and, on certain nights, for dancing; but there were no other professional entertainers, and any further exposure to the performing arts came from within the ranks of guests.

Fortunately, volunteer talent abounded. The management had only to post a notice announcing an amateur entertainment that evening to bring forth a spate of vocalists, tap dancers, elocutionists, magicians and instrumentalists who just happened to have their instruments with them. Actually, you didn't even have to be a guest. If you had friends staying at the Inn, as we usually did, you were cordially invited to attend these evening entertainments and to add your own particular talents, if any.

Nor were the ranks of performers limited to adults. Children, too, were permitted and even urged to take part. Doris, even then an accomplished pianist, was much in demand to render "Voices of Spring" and "The Beautiful Blue Danube" at concerts. And Cousin Alfred and I once won a prize for dressing up in oilskins, boots, sou'westers, beards and clay pipes and carrying clam rakes and pails at a costume party. No modicum of talent went unnoticed.

Evening entertainments took various forms. There were, as noted, concerts and costume parties. There were also readings, stereopticon slides, dances and skits. It was the concerts, however, that brought out the most talent and furnished the most well-rounded performances. The only trouble was that Chequesset Inn guests had a habit of coming back year after year, a custom that lent a certain sameness to the programs. After you had heard Mrs. Frothingham sing "Indian Love Call" four successive summers, some of the first careless rapture went out of her performance.

Some guests had the good sense, or perhaps the ability, to vary their renditions. There was a middle-aged man named Mr. Tower who came each year with his mother. Among his wardrobe he always included a black suit in case it became necessary for him to attend a funeral. This eventuality never came to pass, so far as I know, but a concert provided the next best opportunity to wear the black suit, and Mr. Tower did so each summer.

He was possessed of a powerful baritone which, when in full cry, could drown out even the sound of the waves washing the pilings beneath the pier. His repertoire was somewhat larger than that of Mrs. Frothingham, running largely to robust, masculine numbers. This was surprising, for Mr. Tower was a rather slight man with a Walter Mittyish air.

Although he liked to do the "Erlkönig" song, he was perhaps at his best in "The Road to Mandalay," especially the last chorus when he pulled out all the stops as his sonorous voice lifted into the final "Chi-nah 'cross the Baaaaaay!" But the concert I recall especially of all came on the night that he rendered "Give a Man a Horse He Can Ride" and then, in unfortunate juxtaposition, gave as his encore, "Sailing, Sailing, Over the Bounding Main."

It was always exciting when, from time to time, fresh talent appeared. Such a talent was that of Mr. Mantini, who played the cornet. In fact, rumor had it that he had at one time been a member of John Philip Sousa's band; a tense expectancy gripped the audience as the assistant manager, who doubled as master of ceremonies, introduced him.

"We are indeed fortunate to have with us this evening a newcomer to Chequesset Inn concerts, a true virtuouso who was formerly a member of a well-known band. It gives me great pleasure to present to you Mr. Louis Mantini who will favor us with a concert solo." He didn't actually say that Mr. Mantini had been a member of Sousa's band—but he didn't say that he hadn't, either.

Immaculate in white flannels (of the sort known as "ice cream pants") and a blue serge jacket, Mr. Mantini took his place before us. He chose as his first selection the "Carnival of Venice," leading off with a rippling cadenza. It was immediately clear that a new star shone in our midst.

Mr. Mantini attacked with vigor. If he had indeed played with Sousa, it had undoubtedly been some time ago, but he made up in spirit and enthusiasm for any shortcomings in technique. He wore a luxuriant black mustache, which, with his equally bushy eyebrows, gave him the appearance of

having three mustaches—a small one over each eye and a large one over his mouth. All three came into play as he warmed to his work.

Curiously, when he descended the scale, his mustache and eyebrows bristed upward, whereas flights into higher ranges set mustache and eyebrows adroop. When high and low notes alternated in rapid succession, the effect was to bounce these hirsute appendages up and down in perfect time to the music, a fascinating phenomenon to watch.

When Mr. Mantini came to the triple-tonguing cadenzas of the final passages, eyes and mustache became a blur as notes stuttered in machine gun bursts from his horn and his face turned crimson from his exertions. As the last note drifted into silence, almost hysterical applause burst forth, to which the maestro responded by bowing low and dabbing at his moist face with a silk handkerchief. Unfortunately, Mr. Mantini did not return the next summer, but he left an unforgettable performance behind. If he was not ever actually a member of Sousa's band, John Philip Sousa was the loser.

At least once each summer the help combined their talents to present an evening of vaudeville. A number of the waitresses came from the Sargent School of Physical Education in Boston and these young ladies frequently performed gymnastic feats, attired in middy blouses and bloomers. Other less muscular feminine talent from Radcliffe and Wellesley strummed mandolins or did interpretive dances.

One season the hit of the show was a duet featuring the personable headwaiter from Harvard and the attractive waitress from Mt. Holyoke who sang "Because You're You" from Victor Herbert's *Naughty Marietta*. When the headwaiter came to the line "I just know I love you, dear . . ." he took his partner lightly by the hand and his Adam's apple bounced romantically. They were married the next June after graduation, and the fact that they had met right here at Chequesset Inn furnished porch conversation at least throughout July.

Naturally, such heady pleasures were not inexpensive.

Those who wished to enjoy sea and lake fishing, boating, bathing, tennis, billiards, bowling, orchestra plus entertainments and what amounted to three dinners a day, had to be willing and able to pay the price. The price in 1916 came to $15 a week per person American plan. And, as everyone knew, although the cost of food was going up, a whole family could live for two weeks or more on less than $15. It was clear to Cousin Alfred and me that to stay at the Chequesset Inn you had to be *rich*.

Salt Hoss, Fresh Fish
& Corset Lace

TODAY'S VISITORS to Cape Cod take for granted the profusion of food stores, department stores, drug stores, hardware stores and specialty shops that throng the Narrow Land. It was not always so. Shopping on pre–World War I Cape Cod posed many problems, some of them insoluble.

Take, for example, fresh meat. Once we crossed the Canal on our vacation-bound journey, we said good-bye to roasts and steaks and chops for the duration, for it was difficult in those days to transport fresh meat from city warehouses to the Lower Cape and to keep it fresh once it had arrived.

True, most of the villages contained shops that sold preserved meats and fresh poultry. In Wellfleet it was Davis's Market, run, appropriately enough, by an old salt who in the course of his seafaring life had acquired a wooden leg. I never knew under what circumstances he had lost the original, but it was always interesting to conjecture that it might have been removed, like Captain Ahab's, by a vindictive whale or some other monster of the deep. In any event, it gave him a swashbuckling, Long John Silver look which was enhanced by a piratical gray beard and dark, flashing eyes. Cousin Alfred and I were fascinated by Cap'n Davis.

Incidentally, practically every male over the age of twenty on the old Cape was known as Cap'n. When in doubt, it was always safer to address a man as Cap'n rather than Mister. Usually you were right, even though the craft under the Cap'n's command might have been a quahaug scow.

Cap'n Davis's market was a small, one-room affair that smelled of smoke and brine. Much of its interior, except for the short counter, was taken up by a row of vats. Above them hung thin chickens in various stages of undress and smoked herring impaled through the gills on a stick. Within the vats reposed chunks of long-deceased critters awash in brine, something like pickled specimens in a laboratory.

Cap'n Davis called the contents of his vats "salt hoss," and for a number of years I took the appellation at face value. I am still not really certain. Sometimes (appropriately, it seemed to me) he called it "junk." Father was more euphemistic.

"Do you have a good corned beef today, Cap'n Davis?" he used to inquire.

"Yes, sir," Cap'n Davis would reply. "I got a nice fresh piece of meat for you."

By that he meant it had been in the brine for only a matter of six weeks or so. Picking up a lethal-looking meat hook, he would stump to one of his vats and go fishing about in its briny depths. After a shorter or longer time, he would give the hook a quick yank, like gaffing a salmon, and come up with a battered chunk of dark-colored meat impaled upon its point.

"There," he would exclaim, plopping it down upon the counter. "There's as nice a piece of junk as you'll see this side Buzzard's Bay. Just freshen her up a mite and she'll go down like candy."

Mother learned from experience that if she soaked the

meat overnight and then freshened it in three waters before boiling it for eight hours, it could be rendered edible if not palatable. After a few tries, we gave up on Cap'n Davis's salt beef, but we continued to buy from him chickens and chunks of salt pork for the Saturday baked beans.

We did somewhat better at Wiley's Grocery, which was located on Commercial Street not far from the depot. Mr. Wiley—one of the few citizens who was not a Cap'n—kept his store in a small, white frame building. To its rear was attached a small shed. The shed served as a storage place for the coal, wood and kerosene in which Mr. Wiley also dealt and which gave rich overtones to the mingled aroma of coffee, cheese, apples and molasses inside the store itself.

Up front near the door stood the inevitable candy counter with trays of penny gum and colored candies. The tobacco counter came next, followed by shelves of canned goods, flour, bread, cookies, coffee, tea, sugar, spices, olives, extracts and crackers. A wheel of cheese and a tub of butter sat on the counter beside a red, hand-cranked coffee grinder, and wooden bins of vegetables ranged along the floor below, flanked at one end by a barrel of dill pickles. Rolls of flypaper dangled from the ceiling, well plastered with their victims. Over this mélange Mr. Wiley presided with brisk inefficiency.

Although he had run the store for a considerable time, he could never seem to recall where his various comestibles were located, perhaps because through the years he had allowed the merchandise to intermingle so that the crackers had overflowed into the canned goods section and the flour into that of the bread.

"Now where did I lay them olives?" he would demand,

peering helplessly at the shelves. "I thought they was just astern of the spices."

Ordering from Mr. Wiley followed an undeviating ritual. You would say, "A pound of butter."

And Mr. Wiley would repeat after you, "A pound of butter. Have it."

Not until this confirmation could you go on to the next item. Sometimes I tried to sandwich in two items but to no avail.

"A loaf of bread and a . . ."

"A loaf of bread," he would interrupt firmly. "Have it."

If the order was long, having its various items tracked down and their presence substantiated often required the better part of an hour. Frequently his confidence led him astray. Frequently he murmured, "Have it," only to find that he didn't. Sometimes the item was merely misplaced, at other times it proved to be definitely missing. "But it'll be along on the noon train," he always assured you. Sometimes he was right.

Mr. Wiley sold a rugged cheddar known as "the tasty." Buying it was a ritual, too. Even though you might have purchased a piece from the same wheel earlier, a request for a repeat would bring the invariable question.

"Like it strong, do you?" And without waiting for your reply: "Here, let me give you a sample."

Whereupon, seizing up a sort of cutlass he kept handy, he would carve a quarter-pound slice from the wheel and proffer it to you, along with a handful of saltines. Mr. Wiley's sample was practically a lunch in itself and perhaps it was this practice that made it necessary for him to sell "the tasty" at the steep price of thirty cents a pound.

Stopping off at the candy counter on the way out was always a demanding ordeal. There were soul-wrenching choices to be made among licorice sticks, anise balls, lemon drops, peppermint sticks, lozenges that said Oh, You Kid! and I'm Yours, lollypops in assorted flavors, nonpareils, chocolate or molasses kisses, jawbreakers and gum drops. Sometimes when I felt affluent, I would blow a whole nickel on a bar of Baker's sweet chocolate which Mr. Wiley called "the Caracas."

And, occasionally, on red-letter days, as Cousin Alfred and I took our leave, Mr. Wiley would call after us, "Hot, ain't it? Why don't you boys have a bottle of cold tonic 'fore you go?" And he would let us select from among the bottles of birch beer, root beer, sarsaparilla, ginger ale, Moxie, lemon, lime, orange, raspberry and vanilla soda packed in ice in a big wooden tub.

I always finished my candy on the way home, even though I knew what was going to happen. What was going

to happen was that Cousin Alfred would save some of his and then, at an opportune time, eat it before my famished gaze.

One commodity of which there was no dearth was fish, the freshest and most delicious fish, both salt and fresh water varieties, to be found anywhere. Some species we caught ourselves; for others we depended upon the local fish dealer, Cap'n Lombard.

Cap'n Lombard's close acquaintance with fish went back some forty years to the time when, as a boy of thirteen, he had shipped to sea on one of the several fishing schooners sailing out of Wellfleet Harbor. In this pursuit he had sailed the coast from Baltimore to the Newfoundland Banks, seining mackerel, trawling for cod, halibut, pollock and haddock, depending on the season. When we first met him, he had long since come ashore to sell fish over the counter of a shop rather than hauling them over the gunwales of a boat.

His shop was a small, two-room wooden edifice, the front of which faced on Commercial Street with the rear supported on stilts over a marsh. The front room contained a counter and a case in which he displayed his wares on a bed of ice; the back room, equipped with a wooden block, an iron sink and a large metal "gurry butt" was the site of dressing operations.

Cap'n Lombard's fish came not via wholesaler or broker with days or weeks intervening between water and counter. Instead, they arrived fresh from the sea, firm of flesh and with sparkling eyes on the very day you bought them, or the day before at the most. Long before dawn, first in a horse-drawn van and later in a battered truck, the Cap'n would be on his way to Truro or Provincetown to meet the fishermen as they came in from their traps. Some of their catch was still flopping when lifted from the bins or fish cars. By eight o'clock Cap'n Lombard was back at the shop with his assortment of mackerel, haddock, butterfish, pollock or whatever was in season. He or his son had to travel farther afield, sometimes all the way to Woods Hole, to pick up swordfish harpooned the day before.

At the time, Cap'n Lombard had to charge us ten cents a pound for swordfish, but he could remember when the fishermen used to leave these fish on the dock with a sign on them reading Help Yourself. The price later rose to two cents a pound. Tinker mackerel sold at a price of six for a quarter.

The freshness of his wares was only a part of the rewards of patronizing Cap'n Lombard. The rest was the sheer entertainment value of a visit to his shop. He was an enthusiastic and talented raconteur whose tales became enhanced rather than diminished by the fact that when excited he had a tendency to stutter. Sometimes, owing to both these traits, buying fish from Cap'n Lombard took all morning and we would return home to find Mother waiting impatiently for the fish we had been sent to purchase hours ago.

Tall and angular with sandy hair and a sandy walrus mustache drooping from a somewhat mournful face, Cap'n Lombard was wont to sit asprawl on his counter. Unless the morning was an unusually busy one, he made it clear that he had as much time as you did. His stories ranged from seafaring exploits to equally interesting adventures encountered ashore. One of my favorites was compounded of both.

It had to do with an excursion that Cap'n Lombard and

Uncle Lou Higgins had made to Newcomb's Hollow some years ago in quest of striped bass. Not long after their arrival at the beach, Uncle Lou had a terrific strike that yanked the line from his hands. As an added precaution, he had tied his tarred handline around his waist, and this now threatened to prove his undoing.

"He hove back," Cap'n Lombard related, "but that fish didn't budge. And the next thing he knew, he was being drug into the surf."

At this point Cap'n Lombard unfolded himself from the counter to go into elaborate pantomime indicative of Uncle Lou's desperate struggles to avert his fate. You could see him being dragged relentlessly into the water.

"The line was 'round his knife and he couldn't cast loose. There he was s-skidding on his heels up to his middle in the b-breakers. He hollered like an Injun and I see somethin' was up. I run down the b-beach and grabbed him, both arms around his waist, and dad gum if we both wasn't being hauled out to s-sea. That was enough for me. I yanked out my knife and cut the line just as we were about to go under. I can tell you, that was the b-b-b-biggest b-bass that ever swum this coast!"

He told us, too, of the short period when he had run his fish shop and also a paper store on Main Street. "How on earth did you find time to do both?" Father inquired.

"Oh," Cap'n Lombard explained, "I could always get a woman in m-mornings for a small affair."

Not the least of his talents was that of weather forecaster. Always before planning a beach picnic or other outing that depended upon fair skies, we checked with Cap'n Lombard and he seldom let us down. Many a morning in the midst of a downpour, he would step to the front door of his shop, squint mild blue eyes at the leaden skies and declare, "I b'lieve the wind'll haul around to west'ard on the tide. Ought to clear by midafternoon."

And, sure enough, the wind would swing around, as advertised, to let the sun shine through the scattering clouds. On other days when the sun shone brightly in cloudless blue skies, his dictum would be, "I look for it to clabber up and give us a wetting 'fore evening." And it was even so.

But if he was an expert in matters meteorological, he remained a tyro where modern technology was concerned. To him the telephone constituted a bewildering anathema. Not that the telephone was new. It had been forty years or more since Alexander Graham Bell had summoned his assistant with the famous first message, "Watson, come here; I want you." But Cap'n Lombard still did not fully trust it.

He resisted having a telephone for years, but finally, in an unguarded moment, he suffered his son to have one installed on the wall of his shop. We learned of his distrust of the instrument when we called at his shop to buy lobsters.

Friday was lobster day at Cap'n Lombard's and we were regular customers. But, somehow, on this particular Friday morning, through a foul-up, our order had been sold to someone else. Even more distressing, there was none left in his case. Cap'n Lombard was most apologetic, and it is the measure of · his esteem for Father that he at length volunteered to telephone the Orleans lobsterman who was his source of supply.

"Can you go and get them?" he asked.

"Certainly," Father replied.

"How many pounds do you want?"

"We can use nine pounds," Father said.

"And what time will you pick them up?"

"Oh, let's say two o'clock."

Armed with this information, Cap'n Lombard squared his shoulders, took a deep breath and advanced determinedly upon the telephone. Grasping the crank gingerly, he spun it several times and then picked up the receiver. "Two-t-two-four," he told the operator, "Mrs. Thompson in Orleans."

A moment later, "Hullo!" he barked. "Is this the wrong n-number?"

Despite this defeatist approach, it developed that the lobsterman's wife was indeed at the other end of the wire. This fact having been established, Cap'n Lombard raised his voice to the strident bellow he had once reserved for the poop deck of his schooner. After all, his listener was ten miles away in Orleans and he intended to provide the necessary volume to allow his voice to carry that far.

"I have some p-people who want lobsters," he roared. "Have you g-got some? Yes. Well, they want n-n-n-n— They want n-n-n-n—They want fifteen pounds and they'll be over to get them at t-t-t—at t-t-t—at f-four o'clock."

That was one time I had all the lobster I could eat.

Native lobsters from bay and ocean were plentiful most of the time, but now and again, after a nor'easter had scattered the pots or prevented the fishermen from tending them, they would become scarce for a time. During one of these periods of dearth when neither Cap'n Lombard nor the Orleans lobsterman could supply our needs, we were driving through Chatham when we saw a sign on a shingle cottage beside the sea. Lobsters, the sign read and Father brought the Pope-Hartford to a screeching halt. A sharp-faced woman answered his knock at the door and stood regarding us impassively.

"Do you have lobsters?" Father inquired.

The woman nodded. "Yes, I do," she admitted cautiously. "But they're awful dear."

"How much?"

The woman sighed. "I hate to tell you."

"Well . . . uh . . . I'd like to buy some," Father ventured.

"No, you wouldn't," the woman said. "They're too dear."

"I'd still like to know the price," Father persisted.

"Well," the woman declared hesitantly, "I have to ask . . . twenty cents a pound."

In point of fact, that was indeed higher than the customary twelve cents a pound that Cap'n Lombard charged, but, since they were scarce, Father didn't quibble.

A man named Atwood kept the hardware store. He liked to say that if you asked for a trolley car he could likely lay his hands on one somewhere among his stock. I am not aware that anyone ever called upon him to produce a trolley car, but I do know that he often found it difficult to lay hands on other more common items. In fact, a request for a kerosene lamp or a tack hammer invariably led to an all-out search, in which the customer joined, through garden tools, wire screening, ironing boards, tubs, pots, pans, nails, bolts, screws, kerosene stoves, rope, oil cans, watering cans, washboards, axes, shovels and fishing tackle.

"There you be!" Mr. Atwood would exclaim triumphantly as he came up with the evasive merchandise. "Ain't she a beauty?"

Best of all, to me, was Mr. Atwood's fishing tackle. His

entire stock was contained in a small glass case near the door, but to me it was a fascinating display. It comprised a curious mixture of fresh and salt water equipment for all species of fish from perch up to sharks. Wooden boxes of split BB shot nestled beside pound codfish sinkers, and snelled trout hooks mingled with forged steel hooks on chain traces suitable for drawing out leviathan.

There were green handlines on wooden frames to use in fishing for eels from the town pier and there were coils of tarred line to use in fishing for codfish in forty fathoms of water. There were small red-and-white bobbers and big green-and-white bobbers. There were a couple of nickel-plated bait-casting reels, a spool or two of bait-casting line and five or six lethal-looking fish knives with saw-toothed scaling blades.

But the thing that really took my eye was a card of snelled bass flies hanging on the wall behind the case. There were a dozen of them, gaudy, feathered creations bearing such intriguing names as Lord Baltimore, Lady Baltimore, Yellow Sally and Dark Montreal. At the top of the card was depicted a huge bass showering spray as he leapt open-mouthed in his eagerness to engulf one of these magic flies. I felt certain that if I were to cast such a lure along the pad-bordered shore of Great Pond, I would undoubtedly attract a bass like the behemoth on the card. Mr. Atwood agreed with me.

"They catch bass other places. Ought to catch bass here, seems so," he averred. "Thing is, nobody's tried 'em. Ain't many people fishing the ponds and them that do stick to minnows and shrimps."

Here was an opportunity to be an innovator and a

Simeon Atwood's Store

pioneer. By firmly disciplining myself to avoid Mr. Wiley's candy counter, I was able to purchase one ten-cent fly. I chose a Lady Baltimore and Mr. Atwood nodded approval.

"Ain't she a beauty?" he declared admiringly. "Fish ought to take that, seems so."

One did, too. The first time I tried it in Great Pond, a bass grabbed it, not a monster like the one on the card but a smallish sort of bass. He leapt once and when he splashed back into the water, my Lady Baltimore went with him. The snell had broken off at the hook.

I reported the incident to Mr. Atwood and he was full of tsks. "Well, I swan," he said, and I think he was the only person whom I ever heard actually swan. "Shouldn't have busted like that, seems so."

He picked a Yellow Sally from the card and bent the snell between thumb and forefinger. It promptly snapped and so did a Lord Baltimore.

"Well, now look at that." Mr. Atwood shook his head.

"How long have you had these flies, Mr. Atwood?" I asked.

His brow wrinkled in thought. "Well, I guess now you ask, maybe eight, ten years. Drummer sold 'em to me and said folks would go crazy over 'em. But not many people here fish the ponds."

He offered to refund my dime but I chose a red-and-white bobber and a box of split shot instead. The next time I visited Mr. Atwood's store the remainder of the card of flies had disappeared. The Great Pond bass were safe from innovation.

I had less reason to visit Higgins's Dry Goods Store and was therefore less familiar with its proprietor and his offerings. About the only errands that brought me inside the portals of Mr. Higgins's store were the purchase of a yard of mosquito netting to cover a dip-net or a piece of unbleached muslin to make an awning for a frog. My sister Doris, though, patronized the place frequently, sometimes with unpredictable consequences.

In that earlier day, feminine fashion dictated a figure rigidly restrained—in places—within the fettering confines of a corset. These garments laced up the back, and if a lace broke, the entire contraption abdicated its responsibilities. This unfortunate contretemps had overtaken my sister and on an August day she presented herself at Higgins's Dry Goods Store to buy a new lace.

It was an errand fraught with some tension, for females in those days were less candidly outspoken concerning their underthings, especially adolescent young ladies of sixteen. The subject of corsets was not one to be discussed in mixed company. However, Mr. Higgins was a dealer in ladies apparel and one could mention corsets to him, much as one could discuss other intimate problems with one's family physician. Thus emboldened, my sister sought out Mr. Higgins. Unfortunately, there were a number of other customers in the store, some of them male and, also unfortunately, Mr. Higgins was a bit hard of hearing.

Summoning her courage, my sister announced the purpose of her visit. "I'd like a corset lace, Mr. Higgins."

To which Mr. Higgins replied in a loud voice, "What?"

Pinkening, my sister repeated her request in a slightly louder voice. "I'd like a corset lace."

"Oh," Mr. Higgins said. "This way." And he led her to a drawer which he opened to disclose an assortment of lace. "How about this?" he asked, holding up a piece.

"No," my sister protested anxiously. "Not that kind of lace. A corset lace."

It was Mr. Higgins's turn to protest. "This is the coarsest lace I got," he said firmly.

At this point, completely unnerved, my sister bought the piece of lace and ran home on the verge of tears.

Of all the various stores that comprised the business district of the village, my real favorite was Nye's Souvenir Shop. This designation was something of a misnomer, for while Mr. Nye's emporium did indubitably contain a wealth of souvenirs, its main function was that of ice cream parlor.

The souvenir department was in the front of the store. If you were able to withstand the enticements of the soda fountain at the rear, you could browse through a remarkable collection of memorabilia. Besides the array of picture postcards, Mr. Nye offered polished clam, scallop and quahaug shells, various-sized pillows stuffed with pine needles, figurines of sea captains in oilskins, trays, lamps, ash trays, pen knives, plates, cups and saucers, dolls, glasses, arrowheads, watch fobs, bracelets, rings and a host of other items, each plainly inscribed Souvenir of Cape Cod.

The best browsing of all, however, took place in the room at the rear, a smallish room furnished with a marble-topped soda fountain, a few round, white tables and wire-backed chairs. Placards around the wooden walls depicted some of the delectable "college ices," now known as sundaes, which were just coming into fashion.

Seated in a wire-backed chair at a round white table, you were faced with decisions even more momentous than those encountered before Mr. Wiley's candy counter. If you were insolvent, of course, you had to settle for a five-cent cone or a plate of ice cream. For a dime you could enjoy an ice cream soda. But if your pocketbook (Souvenir of Cape Cod) contained the sum of fifteen cents, a world of gastronomic adventure lay before you.

For fifteen cents you could, of course, order any of the ordinary college ices—strawberry, butterscotch, maple walnut and the like—but you could also indulge in one of Mr. Nye's own fanciful creations, named in honor of local citizens. There was even a menu to help you in your choice, a menu which lovingly set forth the ingredients in each concoction.

Would it be a *"Captain Art Paine*—scoop of vanilla ice cream, scoop of strawberry ice cream, crushed pineapple, strawberry syrup, peanuts, whipped cream, cherry"—or an *"Aunt Martha Special*—scoop of chocolate ice cream, scoop of maple walnut ice cream, chocolate syrup, sliced peaches, sliced banana, walnuts, whipped cream, cherry?" These were decisions that tried one's soul.

Whatever one ordered, Alice, the waitress, would inquire, "Water or soda?"

And you could choose either vichy water, which tickled your nose, or plain water, to sip at intervals as wine tasters clear their palates with black coffee, the better to savor each spoonful of syrup, fruit, nut and cream. Ambrosia.

Pickerel, Perch
& Pout

ASIDE FROM Cap'n Davis's "salt hoss" and chickens, Cap'n Lombard's fish and lobsters and the comestibles we purchased from Mr. Wiley, much of our food we obtained directly from the land and sea as the Pilgrims had done three centuries before us and the Indians before them. And we had about the same choices for our menu—fish, shellfish, berries and vegetables in season.

As the Pilgrims had their faithful Squantum to show them the ropes, so we had our mentor, Mr. Hopkins. It was he who showed us where succulent oysters bedded, how to rake quahaugs from the shallows and where to find fat steaming clams at low tide. He showed us freshwater ponds hidden away among wooded dunes and arranged for our salt water fishing expeditions.

The sea, of course, provided the major portion of our diet, but for variety we turned frequently to the freshwater ponds that dot Cape Cod from Bourne to Provincetown. Henry David Thoreau, one of the Cape's first vacation travelers who visited the Narrow Land in 1849, declared that this multiplicity of ponds derived from an underground river that had its source in the White Mountains of New Hampshire.

An earthquake aeons ago, according to his theory, cracked the flinty pan underlying the Cape, allowing fresh water to gush up to fill the hollows. This is an interesting hypothesis but, unfortunately, one that doesn't hold water, no pun intended.

Present-day science tells us that these ponds were formed by the Great Glacier. As it retreated northward, huge chunks of ice broke away from the main mass to lie like stranded icebergs across the landscape. Slowly, alluvial sand and gravel from the melting glacier's outwash built up around the blocks of ice. Thus insulated, they survived for many years after the glacier's disappearance.

At last, however, they succumbed to the action of the sun on the warming land. One by one they vanished, leaving craters in the sandy plain. To geologists these craters are known as kettle holes. In many cases their bottoms lie well below the water table and ground water has seeped in to fill them, creating ponds. Water lost by evaporation is replaced by that of flowing springs, so that the ponds are actually large natural wells. Some, whose springs pour more water into them than evaporation can take care of, have outlets to salt water.

In any event, well over 400 of them, ranging in size from five up to 750 acres, dot the Cape. Some are sandy-bottomed, others have muddy bottoms beloved of spatterdock and pond lilies. There are said to be twenty-four ponds in the town of Wellfleet, most of them, like the other Cape ponds, well populated with various species of fish including trout, bass, white and yellow perch, pickerel, horned pout and eels. Fifty years ago there were no trout but there were even larger numbers of the other varieties than remain today.

Our frequent trips to the ponds were always red-letter occasions. Not the least of our pleasure derived from the pre-trip activity of obtaining bait. Worms were scarce in the sandy Cape Cod soil, so scarce that we never tried to use them. Instead we resorted to the equally effective grass shrimps and minnows that swarmed by the millions in brackish tidal creeks and by the scores in pools left on the flats at low tide.

There were several ways to hunt this bait, all of them fraught with almost as much excitement as using them later in the actual fishing. The grass shrimp were the easiest to come by. To catch them you had only to sweep a long-handled dip net at half tide gently around the pilings of the railroad trestle below the depot.

These small, transparent crustacea, exact replicas of their larger edible cousins, swarmed in such places and in tidewater pools, and a dozen or so dips with the net would provide enough bait for a day's fishing. Mr. Hopkins showed us how to net them and then to keep them in a bucket under a sprinkling of sawdust.

We used a slightly different technique in capturing the salt water minnows known on the Cape as mummychubs. If you arrived at the trestle at the right time on an incoming tide, you would see an unbroken procession of these small fish schooling in the rising waters of the creek, following closely the contours of the shore. If you placed your dip net in the water with its opening facing the oncoming hordes and let the current hold the mosquito netting bag open, you were in business.

When the net first entered the water, the parade of mummies would explode in a showering silvery spray and then swim around it. But if you left it there quietly for a few minutes, sooner or later a few minnows would enter, followed by those behind. In one scoop you could bring in a hundred or more, ranging in length from one to four inches.

If the tide was not at the right stage for this method to be successful, catching mummies took a little longer. Then you had to use a drop net suspended on a length of tarred codline. You baited the net with a couple of crushed clams and lowered it from pier or trestle.

In a short time the mummychubs would be attracted to the bait. When a dozen or more were busy worrying it, you yanked the net upwards, capturing them, along with an occasional fiddler crab, in its meshes. This method took longer than dipping but was equally exciting. The mummies we also kept in sawdust, and they would be as lively and active at night as they were when taken from the water in the morning.

The great difficulty in fishing the ponds in those days was in reaching them, since most lay hidden away at the end of narrow sand roads that often turned to faint cart tracks. No automobile could possibly negotiate these brush-grown byways winding through scrub oak and pine woods; the only practical means of travel was afoot or by wagon.

For this reason, we concentrated on a half-dozen or so of the larger and more accessible ponds. To some we walked, but for most pond-fishing expeditions we hired a horse and wagon at Holbrook's Livery Stable. This, in itself, was an experience.

The stable had a distinct Currier and Ives look with its weathered boards, its gaping door and the cupola atop its wide, sloping roof. The gloom of its cavernous interior was relieved by light struggling in through dirt-glazed cob-webby windows. The heavy oak planks of the floor had been splintered by the tread of countless iron-shod hooves over the years and there were even wheel ruts in the plank ramp leading to the door. Over all hung a pervasive aroma of ammonia, manure, leather, hay and, by the time I knew the place, gasoline.

For Marty Holbrook and his son Henry had seen the writing on the wall and their stable now served also as a garage. They even had a mechanic who knew how to tinker with gasoline engines. Actually, he had learned his trade working with marine engines, but as he said, it was six of one, a half-dozen the other. As Henry put it, "It's all hoss power, ain't it?"

In those days one never left an automobile outdoors overnight except in cases of dire necessity, especially in damp seashore air. If one did, the car would inevitably fail to start in the morning without extensive and time-consuming ministrations which sometimes included baking vital parts in the oven. Since the Hopkins house had no garage, the Pope-Hartford was one of the Holbrooks' clients.

Most of the Holbrooks' business still centered around horses, but besides the Pope-Hartford, one could see a growing sprinkling of Fords, Simplexes and Packards parked among the buggies, surreys and buckboards of the carriage room. The horse stalls were located in the cellar, and when you ordered a "rig" one of the grooms—there were two—would lead your horse up a winding path to the harnessing room near the big front door.

Cousin Alfred and I never tired of watching the groom as he went about the job of harnessing—slipping the bit between the horse's jaws, fitting blinders, collar, saddle, reins and crupper, and then backing the animal into the shafts to fasten the tugs.

If a sizable group were going on a picnic–fishing excursion to the ponds as occasionally happened—perhaps Doris, Mother and the Hopkins family—we hired a surrey. But if, as was more likely, the expedition was an all-male one consisting of Father, Mr. Hopkins, Cousin Alfred and me, we traveled in a light wagon with Father and Mr. Hopkins on the seat and Cousin Alfred and me perched in the back amidst the fishing tackle, lunch and bait.

One of our favorite fishing haunts was the chain of ponds—Gull, Higgins, Williams and Herring—located between Wellfleet and Newcomb's Hollow. As we turned sharp right from the oiled macadam surface of the King's Highway onto Gull Pond Road, the wheels of our wagon sank deep in soft, white sand.

Shortly the woods closed around us, and when the overhanging branches began to whip against the sides of the wagon it became necessary to button the side curtains. Hog cranberries carpeted the rolling ground on either side and beach plums, bayberries and lowbush blueberries grew thick alongside the dusty road, together with bouncing bet, Queen Anne's lace, choke-cherries and tiger lilies. Branches scritched harshly against the wagon. Crows called above the pines and from the scrub oak thickets came the bobwhite calls of quail. To our nostrils came a warm scent of pine mingled with salt sea air, and as we neared the ponds, we could hear the low, rhythmic beat of surf upon the outer beach.

Always leisurely, the trip took a greater or lesser time, depending on the horse, the day and the driver's mood. Eventually, however, we would top the short rise to see Gull Pond shimmering blue among the pines. Near the shore at its southern end stood our destination, the weathered shingle home of Uncle Ben Eaton.

Chickens fled squawking from our path as we drove into his yard. Their commotion usually brought Uncle Ben from house or barn to greet us, wearing his battered straw hat, smoking his stubby corncob pipe and with his faded gray trousers held up by white suspenders with wide clips inscribed "Hit 'Em Again POLICE."

A short, wiry man in his late sixties, Uncle Ben had been a master carpenter in earlier years and even today he did a bit of building. But mostly he stayed at home, puttering with his chickens and his garden, selling a few eggs and vegetables and renting the two boats he had built some years before. Neither venture could have been lucrative because there were very few customers for his boats and the local fauna annually raised havoc with his garden.

"Them deers," he would declare, shaking his head, "they've et up all my peas and now they're into my beans. It's a caution."

"Why don't you shoot 'em?" Mr. Hopkins asked him one day.

"Oh, I couldn't do that," Uncle Ben protested. "I kind of like to see 'em around. Besides, if they eat the beans it saves me the trouble of picking 'em."

Father and Mr. Hopkins never seemed to be in a great hurry to get to the fishing. Often they lighted pipes and sat in the shade of Uncle Ben's apple trees, solving the problems of the world, or else they made lingering tours of inspection through Uncle Ben's garden, evaluating the progress of his sweet corn and examining the damage done by the deers while Cousin Alfred and I fretted with anxiety.

But at length they would come to the business at hand. Cousin Alfred and I were dispatched to the shed for oars, rowlocks and anchor and with Uncle Ben in the lead we would all file down the path to the shore, laden with our impedimenta.

Uncle Ben's skiffs were named *Unis* and *Una*, and they were usually full of water. "Keeps 'em swoll," Uncle Ben explained as Cousin Alfred and I took turns bailing. They were large skiffs, or so they seemed to me at the time— heavy and a bit awkward but entirely seaworthy when a stiff nor'wester set white caps atumble across the pond.

By tacit agreement Mr. Hopkins usually rowed across Gull Pond. He still retained his native ability with the oars, using the short, quick strokes that mark the deepwater sailor. When he had gone back to the city, we had to make do among ourselves, but when Mr. Hopkins was with us, he sat in the oarsman's seat by divine right.

Father and Mr. Hopkins wore rubber hip boots on these expeditions, but Cousin Alfred and I went barefoot with our khaki trousers rolled to the knees. Together we would shove the boat out into the pond and then clamber aboard, Mr. Hopkins amidships, Father in the stern and Cousin Alfred and me huddled in the bow.

For some reason we never fished in Gull Pond in those days. Why I don't know, because it was well populated with pickerel, perch and horned pout and today is excellent trout water. Perhaps it was owing to its great depth—Mr. Hopkins declared it had no bottom—and the extreme clarity of its shallows which made fishermen more visible to the fish. In any event, we were in Mr. Hopkins's hands and he invariably set his course directly for the sluiceway at the opposite side of the pond.

Gull Pond is almost exactly circular, sandy-shored and bordered by pickerel weed and lily pads. A steep, wooded bluff rises from its western shore with a narrow spit of land separating it from Higgins Pond to the north. Uncle Ben's house stood—and still stands—near the southern end of the pond and to the east a gentle slope rises to meet the high, grass-covered dunes that overlook the sea at Newcomb's Hollow. At the time, Uncle Ben's house was the only habitation in sight, save for the remains of a goose-hunting camp.

As we left the crystal shallows, the deepening water turned a light and then a dark green color as one looked down into its depths. A line of white seagulls always sat in mid-pond, rising at our approach to wheel and settle again when we had passed by. Mr. Hopkins said that in former years great flocks of wild geese frequented the pond as a resting and watering place on their migrations north and south.

Local gunners would visit the pond then in spring and fall

with their live decoys, bagging hundreds of geese, many of which found their way to the Boston market where they brought twenty-five cents apiece. But market gunning had by my day been banned, and, as a result, a few geese were beginning to visit the pond again each year.

Now in summer, kingfishers darted with their raucous rattling cries along the shore, feeding upon minnows in the shallows. Frequently, we would see some of Uncle Ben's deers, perhaps a doe and her spotted fawns, splashing among the lily pads.

The pond is about a half-mile across. Mr. Hopkins told us that at Sunday School picnics held on its shores in his boyhood he and his friend Sam Cobb used to swim across to the sluice and back as a feature of the entertainment.

"Sam was a good swimmer," Mr. Hopkins declared, "but it didn't help him much when the schooner he was mate aboard fetched up on Peaked Hill Bars in a winter nor'easter. Not a man of her crew got ashore alive."

At each crossing of Gull Pond Mr. Hopkins performed an unvarying ritual. About halfway to the sluice he would ship his oars and take from his pocket a collapsible tin cup. Scooping it full of water he would drink with obvious relish and then solemnly proclaim: "I tell you, Doc, that's the best medicine in the world for whatever ails you. If folks could just drink this water every day they'd never be sick again and they might live forever."

The sluiceway that connects Gull Pond with Higgins Pond had been built in some bygone time by the village of Wellfleet in order to allow the spring run of herring up the Herring River into Herring Pond and thence into Higgins Pond to continue their journey into Gull Pond to spawn.

Theoretically the sluice was supposed to be kept open, with a depth of water sufficient to allow passage for the herring. However, the herring fishery had apparently been abandoned here. For years the depth of water in the sluice had been determined by the abundance or lack of rain rather than by action of the town fathers.

Some years it was as dry as the Sahara; other years there would be a trickle of water through it and occasionally sufficient water to float the *Una* or *Unis* through it from one pond to another. This was most unusual, though. Most of the time it was necessary to wrestle the skiff by brute force along the dry or slightly damp seventy-five-foot channel between the ponds. Sweating, straining, panting and perspiring, we would inch our heavy craft along, pausing frequently to catch our breath, until at last its keel grated on the sand bar at the far end of the sluice.

Beyond the bar, the shore of Higgins Pond dropped steeply into twenty feet of water. Unlike Gull Pond, which had a clean, sandy bottom, the bottom of Higgins Pond was a mixture of sand and mud, and its water, while clear, had a brownish rather than a greenish cast when you looked into its depths. Round like Gull Pond, its shoreline was widely bordered by pickerel weed, lily pads and spatterdock. Sedge grass, beach plums and bayberries crowded close to its edge and in midsummer a cloying scent of mingled pond lilies and honeysuckle perfumed the drowsy air.

Father and Mr. Hopkins customarily fished from the boat, anchoring offshore to dunk their baits in likely spots for perch or trolling slowly past the pad beds for pickerel. But Cousin Alfred and I were too impatient to be thus confined. We preferred to wade the weedy shoreline,

varying the fishing with frequent forays in pursuit of frogs and turtles. Also, this mobility gave us opportunity now and again to duck behind some sheltering dune for a few drags at our Sweet Caporal and cornsilk cigarettes.

Our fishing method was direct and to the point. While Father and Mr. Hopkins wielded their fly rods and bait-casting rods, Cousin Alfred and I stood knee-deep among the pads, flailing away with twelve-foot, exceedingly limber cane poles purchased from Mr. Atwood for twenty-five cents apiece. To the tip of each pole was fastened a twenty-foot length of stout braided line. A businesslike hook at the end of the line with a cork bobber about six feet above it completed our tackle.

When fishing for perch, we impaled either a small mummychub or a shrimp upon the hook; then we waded into the pads until the warm water just brushed our knees and cast our baited hook to the deep water beyond the pad beds. The bobber lit with a quiet splash, sending little concentric rings widening around it before it turned upright to float serenely upon the quiet surface of the pond.

Dragonflies, slender metallic shafts of green and blue, hovered above the pads or poised motionless at the tip of our bobbers. Water skaters zigzagged around our bare legs. Turtles poked dark noses through the surface, gulls wheeled high above and to our ears came the low surge and resurge of the surf.

Then, suddenly, a tiny quiver set the cork dancing. It bounced . . . bounced again . . . and plunged beneath the surface. At this point we yanked the cane pole upward to feel solid resistance at the end of the line. The next step was to lay back hard with arms and shoulders, catapulting the surprised fish out of the water in a sweeping arc to land flopping on the shore behind us.

Pickerel were different. If you wanted pickerel you used a large mummychub for bait and you hooked it lightly just under the dorsal fin, allowing it to swim freely just off the pads. Sometimes it swam thus for quite a long time. But usually, sooner or later, the bobber, which had been drifting in aimless circles in response to the mummychub's movements, suddenly began a slow, steady glide toward the pads. This meant that a pickerel had grabbed the bait and was moving off with it. The temptation to yank the pole upward was great, but we had learned that this would most often result in pulling the hook from the pickerel's mouth.

These long, lean fish customarily grab their prey from the side, holding it crosswise in their jaws as they return to their hiding places among the weeds. There they lie quietly, turning their victim lengthwise in order to swallow it. During this period, practiced fishermen such as Cousin

Alfred and I wait with a slack line, for any tension causes the fish to eject the bait.

This leisurely turning process may take from one to three or four minutes, but at some time during it the pickerel will feel the hook or line. Once this occurs, he will dart away in a sudden surge. Then is the time to set the hook—hard. Sometimes Cousin Alfred and I set it so hard that the pickerel came flying through the air, festooned with lily pads. But if, as occasionally happened, the fish was a sizable one in the two or three-pound class, such tactics were impossible. Then you had either to let the fish tire itself against the pressure of the lithe cane pole or else drop the pole, grab the line and hand-over-hand the fish to shore. Cousin Alfred and I used both methods.

Later on, from Mr. Hopkins we learned about another even more effective way of catching pickerel. Once we had caught a yellow perch, we sliced off a thin strip of its belly from pectoral fins to tail. Taking off our bobbers and hooking this strip between the pectoral fins, we would "skitter" it off the pads, moving it along in short, darting jerks which the pickerel could seldom resist. Often we would see their V-wakes streaming through the pad beds as they lunged out to take our baits in a shower of spray.

There were some truly sizable pickerel in the Cape ponds in those days. The largest I ever caught was a five-pounder but Father caught one nearly a pound larger on a cast frog bait. These fish were small, however, compared to a pickerel that one of the crew of the Cahoon's Hollow Life Saving Station caught one winter through the ice of Great Pond. That pickerel, on Mr. Wiley's grocery scales, weighed just under eleven pounds three hours after it was caught. A fellow crewman of the lucky fisherman told Father about the catch the next summer.

"Did he have him stuffed?" Father inquired.

"Yep. Stuffed and baked," his informant replied. "Made a meal for the whole crew."

Since the present record for an eastern pickerel is nine pounds six ounces, it appears that the lifesavers at the Cahoon's Hollow Station ate a world-record pickerel.

From Higgins Pond, another short—and deep—sluice led into Williams Pond, which also contained myriads of perch and pickerel. Often, for a change of scene, we used to move through the sluice to Williams. Doing so was fraught with some anxiety, for on our first visit to the ponds Mr. Hopkins had warned us of a giant black snake that guarded the sluiceway between Higgins and Williams ponds, disputing the passage with all comers.

We had never seen this huge reptile but that was no sign that we wouldn't, and each time I braved the sluice I could feel prickles run up my bare legs. Cousin Alfred and I liked to collect ribbon and garter snakes but a ten-foot black snake as big around as a fire hose, as Mr. Hopkins described this monster, was something else again. We walked warily, peering cautiously into the underbrush on either side. Perhaps the king of the sluice had abdicated, for he never challenged us, but we did see other smaller snakes around the ponds, both blacksnakes and water snakes, all of which gave us a wide berth.

On a bluff overlooking Williams Pond stands the home of John Newcomb, the Wellfleet oysterman immortalized by Thoreau in his book *Cape Cod*. When we first saw the house, the deserted ponds, the deserted ocean beach and the dunes around they looked much as they must have looked seventy years before on the October day when Thoreau came through the Hollow to spend the night at the oysterman's gray-shingled cottage.

After the evening meal, says Thoreau, the old oysterman regaled his guests with stories of the wreck of the *Franklin*, which had come ashore at Newcomb's Hollow in a winter gale the previous year, and of the English steamer *Cambria*, whose shipwrecked passengers roamed these dunes and "played pranks," as he said, with his scoop nets in the ponds.

Williams Pond

Around noon Father and Mr. Hopkins would come ashore and hail us to the sluice between Gull and Higgins Ponds. Here on the sandy beach in the shade of the pines, we ate our picnic lunch, which Mr. Hopkins washed down with cups of Gull Pond water. Or sometimes, if the fishing had been especially good or the day especially fine, we rowed back to Uncle Ben's landing for a cookout on his beach.

Uncle Ben supplied sweet corn fresh from his garden and his wife furnished salt pork, butter and a big iron skillet. It took only minutes to build a fire from scrub pine sticks, a hot fire that burned quickly to glowing red embers, ready to receive the partially husked corn dipped in pond water. While the ears roasted, Father and Mr. Hopkins dressed and fried a dozen or so perch and by the time they had turned golden brown in the skillet, the corn was ready to eat.

And munching crisp fish on the bone and corn on the cob, Mr. Hopkins would glance up contentedly and sigh, "I gorry, Doc, you'd pay fifty cents for a meal like this in a restaurant."

Escoffier was not the only great chef; there were also Father and Mr. Hopkins.

Usually, driving home through the woods, we took time to fill a couple of lard pails with lowbush blueberries for pies that came to the table hot that same night, along with platters of crisp fried perch and pickerel.

Three or four times a summer we made a wider excursion to the Eastham ponds. This necessitated arising early enough to obtain a supply of bait, eat breakfast and arrive at the depot in time to catch the eight o'clock up-Cape train. It took about twenty minutes to make the journey to Eastham. When you stepped from the cindery coach onto the station platform and the train had chuffed away under a plume of black smoke, you could see six ponds spread out around you. All contained perch, pickerel and horned pout, but we usually headed for the largest, called Great Pond. It was only a stone's throw from the depot, and it also harbored an occasional black bass.

Sometimes we fished it from shore, Father and Mr. Hopkins in hip boots and Cousin Alfred and I in our bare feet. Mr. Hopkins was thus engaged when he caught the largest pickerel of his angling career. He was skittering a perch belly on a long cane pole through a pocket in the pads when the big fish hit in a boiling strike. When Mr. Hopkins laid back, his pole bent into a straining arc but the pickerel didn't budge.

A second later it bored deep into the pads, its progress marked by fragments of weeds and leaves rising to the surface in its wake as it threaded through a tangle of stout lily stems. After several attempts to tear the line free, Mr. Hopkins plunged in, clothes and all, and swimming to the battle front, wrestled the tangled mass of pond lilies, pads and pickerel to shore.

"This," he declared proudly, as he stood dripping on the shore, "is the prettiest bokay I ever picked."

The pickerel weighed six and a quarter pounds and remains the largest I have ever seen.

In wandering the shores of Great Pond, I was always intrigued by the ruins of a once-elaborate goose-hunting setup that had belonged to a prominent Boston surgeon. It consisted of a lattice wall about sixty feet long, painted green and thatched with pine boughs and pierced with loopholes spaced six feet apart. At either end of the wall were located pens for the live decoys—the callers, the fliers and the runners. A camouflaged trench ran from the wall to a large, squat gunning camp on the bluff above the shore.

A small tower perched atop the camp and in the old days a guide kept watch from the tower. When a flock of wild geese appeared over the pond, he pressed a button releasing the fliers from their pen. They had been trained to circle the pond, calling loudly, and then to return to the blind where corn awaited them. Meanwhile, the tower man pressed another button alerting the gunners playing cards or yarning in the camp. Grabbing their guns, they hurried through the covered trench to the wall.

By now the flying decoys had usually talked their wild kin into landing, but if they remained too far offshore, the runners were sent out to bring them in. These wing-clipped decoys swam out to mingle with the wild birds and then splashed ashore to receive their reward of corn. Gradually the wild flock followed until it came within range of the gunners behind the wall.

"One on the water and one in the air," was the rule of those old-time gunners and often not a survivor remained after the two quick volleys.

Sometimes, instead of wading the shoreline of Eastham's Great Pond, we used to hire a pair of skiffs from the boat livery. This brought us into close, personal association with its proprietor, Freeman Hatch, who in his way was as fascinating to Cousin Alfred and me as the old goose club, and far more rewarding.

His father, Captain Freeman Hatch, enjoyed the distinction of having sailed the clipper ship *Northern Light* in 1852 from San Francisco to Boston in seventy-six days, six hours, "an achievement," as his tombstone in Eastham cemetery declares, "won by no other mortal." This alone, in our eyes, was enough to shed considerable luster upon the son, but he had facets that made him an individual in his own right.

Free Hatch didn't call his establishment a livery. He called it "Boat Hire" on a weathered gray sign nailed to his dock. But despite the fact that he lived in a simpler day, his instincts were those of a modern marina entrepreneur.

Besides renting boats, he sold bait and a few items of tackle, and, later, gasoline for the first balky outboard motors as they began to come into vogue. And he was far ahead of his time in his sales approach and promotion.

A short, sturdy figure in blue jeans and a jersey, he would stand on his dock, his blue eyes alight behind gold-rimmed spectacles, conjuring up piscatorial fancies that had us aquiver with eagerness to be afloat. None of the modern marina owner's defeatist You-should-have-been-here-yesterday or Too-bad-you-can't-be-here-next-week. To Free Hatch the propitious moment was *now!*

"A fish as long as my leg has been breakin' off the pads this mornin'," he would report. "Shouldn't wonder if he's there now waitin' for you."

"Where, Mr. Hatch?" Cousin Alfred and I would chorus.

"Right off that patch of spatterdock," he would reply, stabbing a stubby forefinger toward the weed-bordered shoreline. "He'll go six pounds if he'll go an ounce."

Or he would observe, "Wind's to the west'ard. That's the best wind for this pond. You ought to really hit 'em today."

And always he was reminded of some prodigious event that had taken place in these waters.

"They's another awful big fish over in the cove—awful big," he'd declare earnestly, gesturing toward the opposite shore. "Broke a feller's pole here the other day." Then, shrugging, he'd add apologetically, "Well, I say the other day. Come to think 'twas two years ago."

If, as occasionally occurred, we came back with a disappointing catch, despite Mr. Hatch's bright promises, he greeted us with mournful mien. "Why-ee," he would declare, sadly shaking his head. "I thought you'd have some fun."

But such contretemps were rare. Usually we returned triumphant, our stringers well filled with white and yellow perch, pickerel and an occasional bass. On one such trip a slightly overweening guest of Father's caught a two-and-a-half-pound pickerel which he pompously held up for Mr. Hatch's admiration. Peering at it dolefully, Mr. Hatch made sympathetic clucking sounds.

"Why-ee," he said commiseratingly, "that's a pretty poor apology for a pickerel, ain't it?"

Not the least satisfying part of a day at Eastham was the return home on the five o'clock down-Cape train, displaying our market basket of fish decorated with pond lilies to fellow passengers with casual determination and then carrying them up the oyster-shell road to the cottage where a hot supper awaited us.

Sometimes we varied our daytime fishing excursions with nocturnal visits to Long Pond for horned pout. These were truly red-letter occasions, entailing the privileges of staying up long past one's bedtime and of being abroad in a magic world of darkness. Our favorite pouting spot was a narrow, sandy, pad-bordered cove nestled at the foot of a pine-covered bluff at the far end of the pond.

A path led to the cove from Cahoon's Hollow Road. As we traversed it in the gathering dusk our smoky lantern's weak beam sent small creatures hurrying off at our approach. Rabbits scuttered into the protecting brush and frogs broke off in mid-croak to plop hastily into the water.

The first order of business was to build a cheerful bonfire

whose leaping flames made shadows dance among the pines and reflected themselves on the quiet surface of the cove. In its glow we baited our hooks with kernels of corn, pieces of minnow, scraps of meat or clam or whatever other comestible came easiest to hand, for the horned pout is practically omnivorous. Sometimes, for good measure, we anointed our baits with oil of wintergreen but this wasn't really necessary.

The procedure was simple. You cast your bait into the deep water of the cove and let it lie on the bottom, held there by the weight of a small sinker. Before many minutes passed, a gentle *tap, tap, tap* vibrating along the line signaled the presence of the quarry. You let him nibble at the bait a moment and then set the hook firmly.

At the prick of the barb, the hooked fish would surge away like a startled flatiron and in those first few seconds would put up a respectable scrap. But his resistance would be brief and shortly, with a peeved grunt or two, he would come slithering onto the sandy shore to be gingerly lifted and unhooked.

On my first pouting expedition I supposed that the fish's two long antennae comprised its horns. I didn't harbor this delusion long but the truth was painfully come by. The horns, of course, are carried as concealed weapons in the pectoral and dorsal fins, and a wound made by any of them is very apt to fester. The approved method of detaching a horned pout from the hook is to run the first and second fingers of one hand up the belly under the pectoral fins while the other gropes and twists in the fish's ample but fortunately toothless mouth. This I learned by trial and error.

Eels as well as pout were grist for our mill and sometimes the fish that grabbed our baits and surged away turned out to be eels, often three feet long and as big around as a man's wrist. Then ensued a frantic chase in the firelight's glow until the slimy creature could be pinned down on the sandy shore and dispatched. Skinned, like the pout, and cut into sections, they were delicious when fried in hot fat, no matter how disconcerting it might be to see the pieces squirming in the pan. The size of our bag was limited only by the length of time we wanted to spend fishing and the number of fish we could use. The only times we caught more fish were when we tried our luck in the salty waters of the bay or ocean.

Few earthly pursuits could be more tinglingly pleasant than to stand beside the still waters listening to the ceaseless chant of a whippoorwill rising above the clamor of frogs while horned pout came ashore in an unending procession and the katydids' insistent cadence stitched the night into a seamless warm blanket sparkling with stars.

Tautog, Bluefish
& Tinkers

ALTHOUGH the freshwater ponds provided diversion and an opportunity to add variety to our diet, it was the sea that truly nourished us during our summers on Cape Cod. The nourishment took various forms and the methods of obtaining it were as widely diverse. One of our favorites was deep-sea fishing.

At the time, Wellfleet Harbor was the home port of a number of fishermen who drew their living from the waters of Cape Cod Bay. Some raked quahaugs from the shallow flats; others fished for tautog, which they iced and shipped to Boston and New York markets. Among this latter group were two native sons, friends of Mr. Hopkins, who contributed to our enjoyment and our sustenance by occasionally taking us on their trips "down the bay."

One of these men was Cap'n Otis Dill, a red-bearded giant who could lift a hundred-and-fifty-pound barrel of fish as easily as I could pick up a shoebox. His partner, Cap'n Oz Lambert, was as thin and angular as Cap'n Dill was stocky and robust. But Oz was wiry and strong and a competent seaman, too. Some years earlier he had served as a crew member on the yacht *Reliance* in its successful defense of the America's Cup.

Their boat, like most of the local fleet, was a broad-beamed catboat converted to power by unstepping her former mast and installing an aptly named two-cycle "make-and-break" engine in the cockpit. The *Dorothy*, as they called her, was not a flashy craft but she was sturdy and did her job faithfully for many years. As Cap'n Lambert was wont to remark when occasionally he scraped her keel against a rock or bumped a mudbank, "She's a workboat, not a yacht. You don't have to pamper her."

Our excursions down the bay began in the predawn darkness with Mr. Hopkins's tap on Father's bedroom window, followed by his stentorian whisper, "Doc! Doc! Four o'clock!"

Father, who had been restlessly awaiting this summons since three, would arise amidst a creaking of bedsprings and pad across the wide board floor to relay Mr. Hopkins's message in equally conspiratorial tones.

"Alfred! Ted! Four o'clock!"

Having heard Mr. Hopkins's original bulletin, Cousin Alfred and I were already scrambling into khaki trousers, shirts and sneakers.

The action moved rapidly to the kitchen where Father clumped about in hip boots, rattling cups, plates and pans as he prepared breakfast. Frequently he would pause in his activities to admonish Alfred and me. "Be quiet or you'll wake Mother."

With breakfast under our belts, dirty dishes carefully stacked in the sink for Mother's later attention and sandwiches stacked beside the thermos bottle, we were ready to join Mr. Hopkins under the paling stars for the half-mile walk to the Town Pier.

There we would find Cap'n Dill and Cap'n Lambert awaiting us, stowing gear in the yellow dory that would take us out to the *Dorothy*. Other shadowy figures moved

through the murky darkness, loading tackle, sacks and quahaug rakes aboard their boats while the staccato *putt-putt-putt* of two-cycle engines drifted across the misty harbor as earlier arrivals headed to sea.

With the well-laden dory listing a bit under the weight of fish cars—small, dory-shaped, wooden boxes bored with holes and with a trapdoor at the top—gear and six persons, Cap'n Dill would row us out to the *Dorothy*, silhouetted against a graying morning sky. While Cap'n Lambert stood in the bow, ready to cast off from the buoy, Cap'n Dill would grasp the engine flywheel in giant hands. The moment of departure had arrived.

Sometimes the moment was agonizingly protracted. The *Dorothy*'s starting mechanism was strikingly reminiscent of the Grey and Davis starter on the Pope-Hartford. When warm, it would often burst into life at the closing of the jackknife switch; cold and damp in the dawn's gray light, it demanded considerable cajolery. Each time Cap'n Dill swung the heavy flywheel, the engine responded with a sullen *Psssst!* and then relapsed into silence.

After about the tenth *Psssst!* Cap'n Dill would start

conversing with the engine, and some of the things he said
to it expanded Father's tire-changing vocabulary. Occasionally the engine refused to start at all. Then Cap'n Lambert
had to summon Ben Paine, the mechanic from Holbrook's
Livery Stable, to work on it.

Usually, though, after a dozen or more turns, accompanied by Cap'n Dill's warming encomiums, it would sigh,
cough, gurgle and snort into a more or less steady chugging.
And we would be off down the bay with Cap'n Lambert at
the helm, Cap'n Dill hovering, wrench in hand, over the
engine, Father and Mr. Hopkins seated on kegs in the
cockpit and Cousin Alfred and I standing proudly on the
foredeck, feeling like a combination of Sir Francis Drake
and Lord Nelson. As we putted out of the harbor, the first
sunrise banners began to streak the eastern sky and a ragged
file of gulls flapped overhead on their way from their resting
place on the bay toward the open ocean.

Our first destination was a sand flat off Lieutenant's
Island where we stopped to pick up bait. Since the dory had
been left tied to the *Dorothy*'s mooring buoy, we had to
anchor some distance off the beach and wade ashore through
thigh-deep water. Cousin Alfred and I prepared for this by
removing our trousers. Then, armed with clam rakes, all
hands splashed through the shallows, loading up buckets
with hermit crabs and quahaugs. When the buckets had
been filled, their contents were transferred to a damp burlap
sack and we were ready to set out once more.

From Lieutenant's Island we laid a course for the channel
between Billingsgate Island and Jeremy's Point. There was
quite a lot of Billingsgate Island left in those days. Its
erstwhile settlement had been abandoned before the sea's

encroachment a score of years before, but there was a harbor called the Horseshoe on whose sandy shore stood a lighthouse and the tumbled-down ruins of several homes, a church and a school. Today the entire island has disappeared beneath the surface of the bay.

Clouds of sea and shore birds—gulls, terns, yellowlegs, plover and curlew—rose as we ran between island and point to wheel and settle again behind us. Rounding the point into the broad expanse of Cape Cod Bay we could see, on a clear day, the slim shaft of the Pilgrim Monument at Province-town and to the west the Manomet Hills blue on the horizon.

Sometimes our destination was Middle Bay Ledge, sometimes the bars off the Truro shore. As we approached the fishing grounds, Cap'n Dill would drop an anchor over the stern and then run three hundred feet or so, paying out line as we went. When he shut off the engine, Cap'n Lambert tossed over the bow anchor fastened to the same line. Then, hauling on the line, he backed the *Dorothy* into position over the fishing area where she was held securely midway between the two anchors.

Now it was time to break out the fishing gear and to toss the fish cars over the side. The tackle was even simpler than the cane poles we used on the ponds. It consisted of coils of tarred handline with a three-ounce dipsey sinker tied a foot or so above the stout forged hook at the end. With a rusty hammer we smashed the quahaug shells and the whelk shells in which the hermit crabs had taken up their habitations and impaled the baits on our hooks, which were then lowered over the side.

At the time, the sandy floor of the bay was carpeted with

a thick growth of eel grass which later mysteriously disappeared. Peering down through twelve to fifteen feet of green-tinted water, we could see occasional patches of clear sand breaking up the expanse of grass, and, if we looked closely, we could make out the blunt snouts of tautog ringing the sandy patches.

The idea was to lower the hook and sinker to the sand bottom of these patches and wait for a bite. Usually it was not long in coming. A quick double jerk would vibrate up the line as a tautog darted from his hiding place in the grass to grab the bait. A sturdy yank of the line would set the hook in the fish's jaw and then we hand-over-handed him to the surface as he surged in powerful lunges from side to side.

Tautog, we learned, have two sets of teeth, one in their jaws and the other farther back in their throats to crush the crabs and clams upon which they feed. Unhooking them requires caution. Once released, they were tossed into the fish cars floating awash beside the *Dorothy*.

The fish we caught weighed from five to ten pounds but some were much larger, and on one memorable occasion I caught a nineteen-pounder that Father had to help me land. This fish weighed only two pounds six ounces less than the present world-record tautog and is the closest I have ever come to catching a record fish.

Sometimes instead of a tautog we brought to the surface a frostfish, sculpin or puffer. The frostfish were good to eat and we carefully placed them aside in a damp sack to take home with us. The puffers and sculpins were cut up for chum.

So through the long summer day we fished while the sun

swung overhead to sink toward the Manomet Hills. When we saw the black smudge of smoke from the noon train streaking the sky along the Barnstable shore, we knew it was time to break out the sandwiches and thermos of lemonade. Up to then we'd been too busy hauling in fish to be hungry.

It seemed only moments after lunch until Cap'n Dill or Cap'n Lambert would glance up from the fishing and declare, "Four-thirty. We better be heading in."

In came the handlines, up came the anchors and we were off across the gently rolling waters, homeward bound with the laden fish cars towing astern. And suddenly came the realization that it had been a long day and that we were tired and hungry. But Cap'n Lambert knew what to do about that.

"Do you boys mind spelling me at the helm for a while?" he would call over his shoulder as we rounded Jeremy's Point.

Tautog

Fatigue forgotten, Cousin Alfred and I would spring to the wheel, one on either side, each of us clutching a spoke.

"Keep her nose aimed at the Congregational steeple," Cap'n Lambert would bid us, and no vessel steered by gyrocompass ever kept more rigidly to its course.

Other boats of home-bound fishermen and qu'augers converged upon us as we approached the harbor and to each we gave a careless wave of the hand, as though piloting a twenty-foot power boat was our customary occupation. In the harbor Cap'n Lambert took over again to thread our way among the anchored small craft while Cap'n Dill stood on the bow, boathook in hand, to pick up the buoy.

On good days—and I can recall no bad ones—the fish cars would be loaded with from three to four hundred pounds of tautog, which, iced and barreled, brought five cents a pound in the Boston and New York markets. That, discounting gasoline and depreciation, brought Cap'n Dill and Cap'n Lambert between $7.50 and $10 a day *apiece!*

As Cap'n Dill said, "It's hard work but there's good money in it."

Not all the catch went to Boston or New York. In return for the money to pay for their gas, our hosts insisted that we take a half-dozen tautog besides the frostfish we had caught. Father and Mr. Hopkins used to filet and salt them and pack the filets away in the ice chest overnight. Next day, freshened and fried with strips of salt pork, they were as tasty as any of the delicacies in Cap'n Lombard's market, and we felt the added fillip of having caught them ourselves.

Something akin to these trips down the bay, but at times even more exciting, were our excursions after bluefish with Cap'n Bunty Newcomb. Cap'n Newcomb was among the early charter skippers and he charged $5 to take a party out bluefishing. It was exorbitant but well worth it when the blues were schooling offshore.

He kept his twenty-eight-foot *Sea Spray* moored in Eastham's Salt Pond close beside the King's Highway. In order to get to the open sea where the action took place it was necessary to navigate the tricky channels of Nauset Marsh on through the harbor and thence to Nauset Inlet, which gave access to the ocean.

Cap'n Newcomb never let Cousin Alfred and me steer his boat, nor would we have dared do so if he had suggested it. Besides the tortuous channels and strong currents, there were tide rips off the inlet and oftentimes a tumbling chop offshore. A short, stocky man with sea-blue eyes squinting from a crinkled leathery face, Cap'n Newcomb was all business and brusqueness, and to Cousin Alfred and me, at least, a bit austere. But he was a good fisherman and capable seaman as well.

Bluefishing, under Cap'n Newcomb's aegis, followed simple and forthright principles. Gear consisted of a coil of tarred codline, a number 4 hook and an eelskin stuffed with a rag. Between whispsawing lines and razor teeth, fingers were strictly expendable and after the first trip I wisely added a pair of canvas gloves.

Sometimes the terns found the fish for us. Watching them whirl like a miniature snowstorm above a patch of violet ruffled sea, Cap'n Newcomb would tell what lay beneath.

"Them's blues!" he'd bellow, squinting against the sun. "See how fast that riffle's travelin'? And the birds— swoopin' an' sheerin' off. They don't dast to argue with a blue."

And he'd yank the throttle wide, heading at full speed toward the wheeling birds while the lines went over the side. Chugging alongside, he'd maneuver his craft to bring the eelskins through the edges of the school and we'd haul in fish as fast and as long as aching arms could take it.

Other times the skipper smelled the presence of bluefish. I thought this was a pleasant fiction but I have since discovered that it was at least partly true, and I have learned the scientific explanation of the feat. Sea water contains countless billions of microscopic organisms known as plankton, upon which baitfish feed. The appearance of a shoal of hungry minnows causes these altruistic organisms to flower in pleased expectancy and this in turn results in their giving off an aroma that has been described as "a cross between a pea soup fog on the Grand Banks and a crate of honeydew melons." A watermelon, Cap'n Newcomb called it.

"I smell watermelon!" he'd roar. "Get your lines over. There's blues around!"

And, almost invariably, the bluefish were there, ripping through the swarming baitfish. Every line towing astern would snap taut and then the idea was to keep 'em coming, giving no slack till they tumbled over the stern to be slatted off on the notched board over the fishbox. There they lay, flipping and snapping, the only fish that, even after it has been caught, will continue to chew anything within reach.

Cap'n Newcomb was continually cautioning us to avoid our quarry's razor teeth. One time, as an example, he told this graphic story, which he declared to be true.

"To show you how these cusses can bite," he related, "I'll tell you about a friend of mine who was fishing these waters a number of years ago. He was trolling with a heavy metal drail and all to once he had a strike that yanked the line right out of his hands and overboard it went. A few days later he was trolling in the same area when he got another terrible hard strike. This time he hauled up a fifteen-pound bluefish. . . ."

"And I suppose you're going to tell us that he found his drail in the fish's stomach," Father suggested.

Cap'n Newcomb shook his head. "No, sir, he didn't. But he found *half* his drail!"

It was a rare day when the fishbox wasn't filled on a tide with additional blues overflowing the deck and spilling into the bilge. They were good fish, too, running from six to

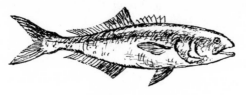

Bluefish

fourteen pounds, but Cap'n Newcomb was always disappointed. He dwelt nostalgically upon the twenty-five-pound bluefish caught at Cohassett Narrows back in '74 and the twenty-seven-pounder that Nelson Elmer hooked off Nantucket as recently as 1903—days when bluefish were really plentiful and catches were reckoned in tons. I didn't believe that, either, but I was sadly to learn of its truth. We were even then in the last years of a bluefish cycle and within a few summers they were to disappear from Cape waters for a number of years to come.

One thing that always fascinated Cousin Alfred and me was the way in which Cap'n Newcomb could hold a lighted match in the wind. Not infrequently, having charged his stubby black pipe with Velvet tobacco, he would scratch a kitchen match on the seat of his corduroy pants and then, no matter how stiff the breeze, instead of putting it to the tobacco, he would hold the lighted match in his cupped hand.

"I'll tell you," he would observe, "there's a slack tide off the inlet now and I don't figure the bait'll be schooling there for another hour or so. I think we'll mosey down Monomoy way and see what's doin' there. Let's get the lines in and sashay right down."

And only then did he bring the match to his pipe and ignite the tobacco with several quick puffs.

In vain Cousin Alfred and I practiced this feat of magic with our cigarettes behind the Hopkins barn. In even the mildest zephyr our match flames would flicker and die before we had spoken three words.

Another wondrous attribute evinced by Cap'n Newcomb was his faculty for always knowing exactly where he was at sea. I recall one day when a fog rolled in from offshore, enveloping us in a thick, gray blanket. Nothing daunted, Cap'n Newcomb continued to run north along the coast as though we were cruising in bright sunshine. Suddenly, he throttled down the engine and circled seaward.

"We're off the inlet," he explained, "and I don't want to run through agin the tide in this fog."

We circled for half an hour or so until, all at once, the fog drifted away to reveal Nauset Inlet dead ahead less than a mile away.

Another time, out of sight of land, Father asked him casually in which direction Boston lay. Scanning sky and empty horizon, Cap'n Newcomb jerked a thumb over his shoulder. "From here," he stated, "she lays nor' nor' west by west half west."

Later, knowing approximately where we had been fishing, I laid compass and protractor on a map and drew a line to Boston. As I had known he would be, Cap'n Newcomb was accurate to the nth degree.

On still other days we sometimes went with Cap'n Manuel Silva, another friend of Mr. Hopkins, when he tended his fish traps off the bay shore of Truro. These excursions began even earlier than our tautog trips down the bay, for Cap'n Silva wanted to be back at the Truro pier by seven o'clock in order to sell his catch to Cap'n Lombard and other market men who were on hand to meet his boat. To go out with Cap'n Silva it was necessary to be on hand at the dock at four o'clock.

Cap'n Silva had the largest boat of all, a forty-footer rigged with a donkey engine and other hauling equipment, with a broad, open deck divided into storage bins for the fish. A small wheelhouse rose aft and a companionway led to the engine room below. To Cousin Alfred and me the *Maria* was comparable to the S. S. *Rotterdam* whose picture hung on our dining room wall.

The *Maria* carried a crew of two besides the skipper. One of them served as engineer on the way to and from the traps and when Cap'n Silva struck a small brass bell in the pilot house for his helper to start the engine, I always had the feeling that I was embarking upon a trans-Atlantic voyage. Actually, the weirs were not very far from shore, although they were located some distance up the coast toward Provincetown.

As a matter of fact, a single strand of net, called a leader, ran from the trap practically to the beach. Fish finding this obstacle barring their path tended to swim alongside it toward deep water. This led them eventually to the circular weir, buoyed at the top, weighted at the bottom and supported by stakes driven into the bottom every twenty feet or so.

The trap was arranged so that the farther the fish swam through a labyrinthine passage, the nearer they came to the huge inner chamber where they were trapped by the scores—mackerel, butterfish, hake, whiting and other species. An intricate arrangement of ropes enabled the bottom of the central chamber to be pursed so that its contents could be emptied into the *Maria*'s bins.

Occasionally a giant bluefin tuna weighing several hundred pounds would blunder into one of the traps and proceed to tear it to pieces in his efforts, often successful, to escape. I recall one such morning when a huge tuna—known as a hoss mackerel to Cape Codders of the day—made horrid inroads in one of Cap'n Silva's traps.

It didn't escape, although it enabled several scores of mackerel and butterfish to do so—but became inextricably entwined in torn netting, floats, sinkers and cordage. Instead of being pleased at the capture of this great fish, Cap'n Silva flew into a gesticulating rage, screaming imprecations in Portuguese and then adding something about being "the son of a beach." He and his helpers fell upon the luckless tuna with knives and axes and, after killing it, let it float away upon the tide.

In those days, tuna were considered worthless and it seems strange to reflect that that same tuna in today's market would have enriched the *Maria*'s crew by some hundred dollars or so.

On most days when the net was pursed, a boiling, foaming, glistening melee of silver fish showered spray as they were drawn alongside the *Maria* and unceremoniously dumped into the bins. When Mr. Hopkins was along, he provided Cap'n Silva with a crew of three, for he hauled lines with the rest, wading knee-deep in fish.

When we returned to the Truro pier, a little group of trucks and wagons would be lined up at the shore end with their owners anxiously waiting to buy the catch. Squid to be used for trawl bait went to the cold storage freezer plant, along with any fish that weren't sold to the market men. Each member of the crew was allowed to take home as many fish as his family could use and the same privilege was extended to us.

"Take tinker mackerel," Cap'n Silva used to urge. "They are the best. Take home and cook for breakfast."

And often we did just that.

Another staple that the sea provided bountifully during our Cape Cod summers was steaming clams. There were a number of places where one could dig them—Billingsgate Island, Jeremy's Point, Great Island, Logie Bay and Chequesset Neck, to name a few. But the real El Dorado, the mother lode of clams, was located on the Truro flats.

We used to park the Pope-Hartford beside the Truro depot and set out, buckets in hand, across the ridged sandbars. Sandpipers, feeding industriously upon sand fleas and other minute crustacea, ran ahead of us as we splashed

barefoot through warm tidal rills filled with tiny crabs and skittering mummychubs. Yellowlegs darted across our path whistling their triple-note cries while gulls and crows flapped overhead in search of carrion left stranded by the tide.

The entire expanse of wet sand was flecked with the bleaching shells of clams, and tiny geysers of water from their living relatives spurted up at practically every step. There was no need for a clam hoe. All you had to do was squat and start a small hole with your hands. Immediately, some four or five inches below the surface, you would strike clams, and, widening the circle as you went, you could dig a bucket in less than fifteen minutes.

You could if you dug steadily, that is. But there were too many distractions to lure your attention from the business at hand. There were white sails on the blue bay, the flight of ducks overhead, the sight of a ferocious-looking goosefish with wide, tooth-studded mouth cast up by the tide, the glimpse of an eel in a tidal rill or a flight of curlew across the flats.

We had to compete with the commercial men who were

allowed to take a two-wheel cartload of clams per tide—and did—but there were plenty for all. Cousin Alfred and I always dug an extra bucket apiece, which we sold to summer cottagers for fifty cents, thus turning a handsome profit.

Today as I pay seventy cents a quart for steaming clams, I recall the days when I sold a ten-quart pail for fifty cents and realize that I was born at least thirty years too soon.

Twenty, Go Thirty

PRESENT-DAY visitors to Cape Cod often wonder aloud how early vacationers amused themselves before golf courses, boutiques, tennis courts, cocktail lounges, drive-in movies, nightclubs, driving ranges and other embellishments of *la dolce vita* came to the Narrow Land. The answer is that they did very well, for, actually, there were just as many activities available then as there are today. Then, as now, one could swim, eat, drink, shop, dance, go to the movies, even play tennis; but it is true that there was a difference.

Take, for example, swimming—or bathing, as it was more usually and perhaps more aptly described. This activity was carried on almost entirely in the clear, unpolluted waters of Cape Cod Bay along the unlittered, uncrowded strip of beach that stretched from Provincetown to Sandwich. There were literally miles of this strand upon which one could spend days on end without seeing another person, except for an occasional clam digger or fisherman. The popular beach areas were located close to the villages, usually within easy walking distance.

Tides affected bathing on the bay side, uncovering wide expanses of redolent mud flats at low water, so swimming was limited to the hours just before and after high tide. No one swam in the numerous ponds, for no person in his right mind would journey several hundred miles to the seashore to bathe in fresh water. Besides, as everyone knew, salt water is salubrious.

About three hours before high water, the earliest enthusi-
asts began arriving at the town beaches, and the incursion
continued until perhaps as many as seventy persons might
be gathered on a half-mile stretch of sand. There were no
bath houses, no life guards sitting in towers, no food
concessions and no fees. You wore a bathing suit (covered
by a bathrobe) to the beach, your safety was your own
responsibility and if you wanted food, you brought it with
you in a picnic basket. Beach umbrellas had not yet been
invented, but occasional parasols gave shade to their owners.

Umbrellas were hardly necessary, though. In those days
one went to the beach to bathe in the water, not the sun,
which was regarded more as a hazard than a benefit.
Sunshine was not considered salubrious. As a result, every
precaution humanly possible was taken to prevent its rays
from reaching any portion of the human anatomy. Both

males and females wore turned-down sailor hats, wide-brimmed straw hats and other headgear designed to protect their heads and faces.

Modesty combined with solariphobia to swathe human forms of both sexes into something more or less resembling mummies. Men and boys wore two-piece suits with sleeves halfway to the elbow and trunks hanging loosely below the knee. Girls and their mothers arrayed themselves in corsets, chemises, puff-sleeved, full-skirted bathing dresses, stockings, bathing slippers and frilly caps. Some wore gloves.

Within this framework some individual touches were permitted. Almost all bathing attire was black, but a woman might have white lace cuffs on her sleeves or even a polka dot dress, and a man might indulge himself by wearing a striped jersey. Such a suit was one adopted by a short, roly-poly gentleman whom we used to call the Michelin Man after a tire advertisement of the day which depicted a human figure made up of tires of various sizes. Our Michelin Man affected a suit composed of wide black-and-white stripes which his natural protuberances formed into a passable imitation of inflated tires.

It was his custom to plunge into the water, carrying his bathing cap clenched in one fist. After immersing himself, he would swim out forty or fifty feet and then roll over onto his back. Taking a big cigar and matches from his bathing cap, he would ignite the cigar, put on his cap and for the next thirty minutes float peacefully awash in the calm water, puffing contentedly and looking from a distance not unlike a spouting whale.

With the elaborate and enveloping costuming in vogue at the time, girl-watching was a somewhat unrewarding activity—and yet perhaps trying to imagine what lay beneath may even have added piquancy to the sport. At the time, however, this purusit was of secondary importance to Cousin Alfred and me. We preferred to give our attention to the Michelin Man and to the well-preserved octogenarian who did headstands on the beach.

It was our unvarying custom, shared by my sister Doris, to leap into the water upon our arrival at the beach and to remain in it until the last possible moment. That was when, having been parentally checked several times for blue lips, we were finally firmly ordered ashore to wrap up in bathrobes and towels to dry off before beginning the homeward trek.

Meanwhile, we had taken turns ducking one another, diving for stones and sea shells, racing each other to the buoy and floating on the gentle waves. Doris, though encumbered by a superfluity of garments, still managed to swim long distances along the shore. One of her favorite courses was the mile stretch of shore from the Town Pier to the Chequesset Inn and back. Out there, alternately stroking and floating, she would reflect upon her absent boyfriend and compare him with the Andover boy she had met at the Post Office last week.

Not for Cousin Alfred and me the long, meditative swim. We preferred fast sprints, somersaults and riotous splashings with other youngsters under the watchful eyes of parents who sat chatting on the beach. Having at last come ashore with chattering teeth, we engaged in building sand castles and tunnels until dry. Then we all trooped back up the oyster shell road to our cottage, stopping en route at Uncle Jim Rich's for an ice cream cone.

Uncle Jim's shop was a room in his small Cape Cod house near the beach. There was nothing fancy about it except the ice cream that he and his wife made in hand-cranked freezers out of eggs and real cream flavored with vanilla, chocolate or strawberry.

The wide ocean beach from Race Point to Monomoy remained almost completely deserted and entirely devoid of bathers, for everyone knew that to venture into the Atlantic surf was to court death from the relentless undertow. If any there were who were not cognizant of this fact, they were soon apprised of it by the ubiquitous life-saving service.

Since it was practical to reach the Atlantic beaches only over roads leading to the life-saving stations, the potential swimmer was always under the watchful eye of the lookouts and beach patrolmen of the service. And if they saw you preparing to swim they would hail you via speaking trumpet and firmly veto your plans. You could, however, paddle in the wash of the surf with your trousers rolled up to your knees. I often wonder what those old-time life savers would think if they could see the thousands of men, women and children daily disporting themselves in the surf of the ocean beaches from Provincetown to Chatham throughout the summer months.

Several times during the summer the *Cape Cod Item & Bee*, which came out on Thursdays, carried advertisements for "vendue sales," by which was meant auctions. These were no ordinary affairs by which householders sought to rid themselves of unwanted junk. Most of them represented, rather, the breaking-up of long-established homes through the death of their owners. A number of them included the property and effects of sea-faring men who had circled the globe in the sperm whale fishery or had sailed great clipper ships in the China tea trade.

Typical is this advertisement from the *Bee*: "Vendue Sale, August 10, 1919. At which will be sold the household furniture, furnishings, utensils and personal possessions of Captain Ora Cobb, late of Andrew Harding Lane, Chatham, including plates, china, glassware, rugs, tools, chests, chairs, beds, chamber pots, cutlery, kitchen utensils, linens, bedspreads, tables, silk bolts, laces, fireplace equipment, stoves, lamps, garden implements, fishing tackle, books, pictures, shotgun, decoys, brass kettle, African mask and weapons, carved box, ivory chess set, Swiss music box and other items too numerous to mention. All guaranteed to be the personal property of Captain Ora Cobb, deceased. Sale will start at ten A.M. sharp, rain or shine. Ambrose Nickerson, Auctioneer."

Occasions such as this were eagerly noted, and young and old, visitors and natives alike flocked to attend, as much for entertainment as with any thought of acquisition. You could always tell when you had arrived at the scene of activities by the big, red flag prominently displayed, the age-old symbol of the auctioneer's trade, and by the cars lining both sides of the elm shaded street and filling the impromptu parking lot behind the house.

It was best to arrive a little ahead of the scheduled starting time, for then you could wander about, inspecting the merchandise to be placed on sale. On sunny days a mingled smell of dust and crushed grass hung in the sultry air as shirtsleeved men and shirtwaisted women in wide bonnets filed past the heaped-up goods and gathered in little groups to chat.

Some auctioneers had their own folding chairs, and those

who didn't borrowed them from the local undertaker so there were always places to sit when you got tired. As the starting hour approached, knots of people drifted to the seats, usually a scattering of dealers and dyed-in-the-wool collectors in the front row, with groups of other men and women, mostly older people, filling in behind them. Many of the women knitted or crocheted as they waited and blue smoke from the men's cigars and pipes hung in the still air.

Promptly at ten the auctioneer mounted the platform to begin the sale. Sometimes it was William Newcomb from Wellfleet, or sometimes Samuel Atwood of Dennis or Ambrose Nickerson of Yarmouth. Mr. Newcomb was our favorite, perhaps because we knew him better than the others.

He was a tall, thin man with sparse black hair combed over a bald spot, a hollow-cheeked, lugubrious countenance and a prominent Adam's apple, which tended to bounce when he warmed to his work. He would bring the short stick that he used for a hammer down upon his portable lectern-like stand with a sharp crack and gaze out upon his audience with a sorrowful expression.

"I declare this sale officially open for business," he would intone and then add, "I can tell to look at you folks that you've got plenty of money and you can tell to look at these goods that they're worth buying so let's get together for our mutual profit and enjoyment."

He usually began by telling a little about the family whose possessions he was auctioning and the events leading up to the sale. Then he'd put up some small item just to start things off. Frequently he would begin with a "Klondike," as he called it.

"Ladies and gents," he would announce, "I'm going to launch this sale with a very useful object—a ten-quart bucket. Just the thing to take out clamming on the flats. And, of course, when you go clamming you'll want a clam hoe, so I'll just drop this short-handled hoe in the bucket like so. Now maybe you got a bad back and you'd rather have a long-handled clam hoe. All right, I'll drop this long-handled hoe in the bucket, too. Maybe some of you can get the little woman to help you dig. One hoe for you and one for the Missus. Now, what am I offered for this complete clamming outfit? Do I hear a dollar . . . do I hear seventy-five cents just to set the ball rolling?"

The first hour or so was devoted to the sale of small, low-priced items to get the crowd into a buying mood and to pass the time while late-comers arrived. It was this part of the proceedings that provided opportunities for Cousin Alfred and me. Cautiously investing our hoarded resources, we were able to acquire a wonderful array of treasures that no one else wanted.

"Now, folks, this jackknife is a rare old ancient antique. The small blade's busted but the big blade—the whittling one—is just as good as new. Who'll give me a dime-dime-dime-dime . . . *sold* to the boy in the sailor hat."

On one occasion when Cousin Alfred and I both coveted a folding tin cup we grimly and recklessly bid against one another until the winner finally paid twice what the cup had originally cost. After this contretemps we learned to let whichever one of us had made the original bid have the item in question and then dicker privately later.

Most of what we bought was worth no more than the fifty cents or occasional dollar we paid for it, but now and again we picked up items of some intrinsic value, among them a bronze harpoon which had buried its barb in who knows how many whales in the far corners of the earth and which for many years adorned my room at home.

By the time the inexpensive small odds and ends had been sold Mr. Newcomb was in voice and going strong.

"Come on, folks," he would cry. "Don't just set there looking at this beautiful Windsor chair. Make me an offer, someone. You 'mind me of Uncle Billy Cahoon over to Yarmouthport. They tell that when Billy was in the Navy his chief petty officer lined him up with some other fellers on the foredeck and sings out, 'Men, I've got a nice easy job for the laziest man in this squad. Will the laziest man step for-ard?' Right away everyone stepped for-ard, all but Billy. 'Why don't you step up with the others?' the petty officer asked. 'It's too much trouble,' says Billy.

"Now I know it isn't too much trouble for some of you to bid on this genuine Windsor chair. Who'll start her off at fifteen dollars . . . fifteen . . . fifteen I got. Who'll make it sixteen?"

As bidding and Mr. Newcomb warmed up, he would break into impromptu chants, his Adam's apple bouncing rhythmically as he mopped his perspiring forehead with a red bandana handkerchief.

"Aydle, beedle, ceedle, deedle, Who'll be first to thread the needle?" or, holding up a bolt of silk, "Bid on this as much as you hafta, This is genuine silken taff'ta."

By noon Mr. Newcomb had worked his way through the minor items and was well embarked upon the sale of the more expensive merchandise. The most important pieces were held until afternoon, but Mr. Newcomb was ready for

a rest before undertaking their disposition. So at twelve
o'clock selling was suspended and the church ladies took
over to feed the assemblage.

It might be the Ladies Aid, the King's Daughters or the
Isabellas who accepted this responsibility, but in any case
the menu was identical. It invariably consisted of ham,
potato salad, cole slaw, rolls, fruit gelatin, cake and coffee,
and it cost twenty-five cents.

Tables made of planks resting on sawhorses were set up
on the lawn and covered with sheets torn from a roll of
brown wrapping paper. On rainy days tent flies fashioned
from old sails covered the proceedings.

Following intermission the sated audience wandered back
to their chairs for the afternoon session. This was usually the
point at which Cousin Alfred and I, now long out of our
financial depth, grew bored. We hung about the commis-
sary department until the last papers had been stripped from
the tables, and then went off to explore or to haggle over the
disposition of our acquisitions.

But, conversely, this was the time to which Mother,
Father and Doris had been eagerly looking forward. This
was the time when Doris could look for linens, flat silver
and tea cups for a nebulous hope chest, and when
worthwhile antique furniture might be acquired for our
home. The trouble was, the dealers bid determinedly among
themselves for all the best pieces, and no one could compete
against them.

They would even go to seventy-five dollars for a pine
chest of drawers! But once in a while, if they had spent
recklessly earlier, you could outbid them on a choice piece.
And on one memorable occasion Father swatted at a
mosquito and found himself the owner of a candle stand

at thirty dollars. At the time, Mother thought this an outrageous price—until a dealer offered forty dollars for it.

Usually, though, the bidding took place entirely among the dealers in the front row and often it waxed fast and furious.

"Now, folks, I'm proud to offer this fine eighteenth-century cherry desk. You've all had a chance to look at her and you've seen her condition. Let's start this off at twenty dollars. Who'll give me twenty?"

"Twenty."

"Twenty, go twenty-five. Twenty, go twenty-five. Twenty-five I have, go thirty, twenty-five, go thirty. . . ."

"Twenty-seven."

"Twenty-seven I have. Go thirty, go thirty, go thirty. . . ."

"Thirty."

"Thirty, go thirty-five. Come on, folks, this is a dandy. I've got thirty. . . ."

"Thirty-three."

"Thirty-three, go thirty-five. Do I hear thirty-five? Thirty-three I have. Going once, going twice—how 'bout it, Henry? All right, going three times and *sold* to Jim Hudson. You got yourself a good buy there, Jim."

Incidentally, I recently saw in a Cape Cod antique shop a cherry desk that carried a price tag of $2,500.

Almost as exciting as auctions and even more rewarding in a material sense were the church fairs held each summer the entire length of the Narrow Land. They were much of a piece, dependent upon the skill in craftsmanship and culinary abilities of the women who conducted them. These were, in all cases, of a high order.

On the day before the event, the men of the church carried tables and chairs to the lawn, hung Japanese lanterns and set up booths decorated with red, white and blue bunting. At that point they retired and the distaff side carried on from there.

When you arrived, you found yourself literally surrounded by a plethora of attractions that made it almost impossible to decide which to give your first attention. The best way was to start at one corner of the hollow square of booths and work your way around the various exhibits.

Most popular of all was the candy booth presided over by two ladies, invariably stout, who sat surrounded by delectable displays of chocolate fudge, penuche, divinity, and molasses sticks. Armed with a box of homemade candy you were ready to make the rounds of the other exhibits.

Almost as popular was the booth displaying baked goods. Fresh loaves of white, brown, whole wheat, graham and oatmeal bread were flanked by mounds of Parker House rolls, White Mountain rolls, baking powder biscuits, blueberry muffins and corn muffins. Close beside them ranged rows of pies—chocolate, apple, blueberry, cocoanut cream, custard, lemon meringue, peach, banana cream and pineapple, along with tarts of the same fillings.

Next to the pies came the cakes—chocolate, fudge, fig, butternut, orange, marble, pineapple, sponge and angel food with cupcakes of similar varieties and cookies of all sorts from brownies through ginger to vanilla. Sometimes, if you had finished your candy and still looked hungry, the ladies would sell you a cookie to eat as you wandered along.

Some baked-goods booths also offered doughnuts, including chocolate, sugared, spiced and plain, round or crullers.

And always, at the back of the booth stood a large earthenware pot of baked beans.

My interest and that of Cousin Alfred flagged somewhat after we had passed the baked goods booth, but Mother's and Doris's enthusiasm remained high as they went on to inspect the booths displaying aprons, needlework, hooked and braided rugs, knitted ware and quilts. They lingered long and lovingly over crewel embroidery and beaded bags, petit point and macrame, and Doris usually ended up with a flowered apron or a dish towel to add to her hope chest.

The ladies were enormously proud of their handicraft as they were also of their canned goods—beans, asparagus, corn, tomatoes, peaches, pickles, jellies and jams—all displayed in neat rows of glass jars in their proper booth.

Cousin Alfred's and my interest became rekindled when we came to the Pirate Treasure Booth. Here, for ten cents, you could select from a large pile of mysterious boxes of all shapes and sizes, wrapped in white paper and tied with ribbons. Having made your choice, you might find that you had purchased a bright-colored felt pen wiper, a scallop-shell ashtray, a paperweight, a bud vase, a bottle of hair tonic, a shoe horn, a bag of sachet powder, a clothes brush or "other items too numerous to mention."

The fascination was more in anticipation than fulfillment, for once you had opened the package you were usually disappointed. But these pirate treasures served a useful purpose as trade goods—a pen wiper and a shoe horn for a change purse.

Another exhibit worth close inspection was that contained in the Souvenir Booth. The souvenirs had all been handmade by some of the more creative ladies and consisted of all manner of intriguing artifacts. One popular seller was a leather wallet with Cape Cod scenes branded on its sides. Another was a bouquet of pine cones tied with red ribbon, and one could find bracelets composed of small seashells, beaded watch fobs and papier-mâchè replicas of Highland and Nauset lights. There were, of course, pillows filled with pine needles, and earrings, necklaces, bracelets and rings fashioned by those accomplished in metal working.

Also worth a glance was the Toy Booth, although its wares were definitely aimed at the infant and toddler sets. There were all manner of rag dolls, stuffed animals, rattles and bean bags and very few air rifles, baseballs or bats. Doris seldom failed to acquire a new stuffed animal to add to the expanding menagerie that covered her bed—eccentric behavior, as it seemed to Cousin Alfred and me, for one who had attained the awesome age of sixteen.

Having made the rounds of the booths, it was time to line up in the queue in front of the tent decorated with black cats and half moons wherein the local fortune teller revealed your future. She was always young and pretty, clad in a colorful gypsy costume with a bright kerchief covering her dark hair (who ever heard of a blonde fortune teller?). Her props consisted of a glass fish-trap float which doubled as a crystal ball, and sometimes a pot of incense.

The only trouble with visiting the fortune teller was that you had to enter her tent alone and sit down at a small table facing her and then suffer her to hold your hand. It was embarrassing, although somehow scarily titillating, to sit thus holding hands with a strange lady even older than your sister.

To make matters worse, she would use the index finger of

her free hand to trace the lines of your palm in the conduct
of her investigations into your future. But it was well worth
it to know that you would have a long and happy life, that
you would become extremely wealthy, would travel widely
and would marry a beautiful girl and live happily ever after.

By the time you left the fortune teller's tent—perhaps
because of the emotional impact—you were invariably
hungry and the refreshment booth loomed as a welcome
oasis. Here, working side by side with the ladies, the only
male participant in the conduct of the fair presided over the
hot dog grill.

Sometimes the grill was a charcoal brazier, sometimes an
oil stove topped by a large iron skillet. In either case, its
attendant was a man dressed in chef's hat and apron. At
frequent intervals he harangued passersby in tones intended
to simulate those of an amusement park barker.

"Red hots! Step right up, ladies and gentlemen. Get 'em
while they're hot!"

While he cooked frankfurts and passed them out on rolls
with mustard and relish, his harried helpers kept busy
handing out coffee, milk, soda and ice cream.

Sometimes, if you had any money left after enjoying the
treats of the refreshment booth, you could make one more
quick visit to the Pirate Treasure Booth or the Candy
Booth. But soon, full of cookies, hot dogs and soda,
clutching boxes of candy, baked goods, doilies, souvenirs
and Doris's stuffed animal, it was time to steer the
Pope-Hartford homeward through the quiet summer dusk.

Saturday was baseball day on Cape Cod, and throughout
the summer rivalry among the teams and their loyal fans,

natives and summer residents alike, was as fanatical as that displayed by partisans of the American and National leagues—perhaps more so. No Cape village was so small as not to support a team of sorts, and sometimes the smaller communities fielded extremely competent nines. For several years Wellfleet had one of the best.

On days when home games were played on the diamond close beside the bathing beach, hand-lettered signs blossomed in store windows throughout the village: CLOSED. Gone To The Ball Game. Everyone in town from six to ninety gathered to cheer on the home team.

Besides the league games, there were usually a number of exhibition games played between the Cape teams and teams from the warships of the Atlantic Squadron, based in Provincetown under the command of Admiral Robley "Fighting Bob" Evans. These games were strictly for blood and occasionally it flowed freely when husky qu'augers made a close play at third against tough sailors.

The climax of these contests came during a summer just prior to World War I when the Wellfleet team, which had won the league title, met and defeated a team from the U.S.S. *Ohio*, champions of the fleet. In a spirited pitcher's battle, Wellfleet won 4–3 and the town celebrated for days thereafter. There may have been no connection, but Admiral Evans never brought the Atlantic Squadron to Provincetown again and the jubilant Wellfleet rooters thought they knew why.

Perhaps the most eagerly awaited of all were the monthly excursions of the C.C.C.C.—the Cape Cod Clam Chowder Club. Its insignia, which each member proudly wore, was a white steamer clam shell with the five C's inscribed upon its concave side.

There were some twenty-five members, recruited from among townspeople and summer residents, and to convey the membership from the Town Pier to Billingsgate Island where the festivities took place, Cap'n Gus Howe put himself and his boat *Cultivator* at the club's disposal. The *Cultivator* was forty feet long with a broad open deck, a pilot house aft and a small engine room below. During eight months of the year she was an oyster boat working the beds in Wellfleet Bay.

In early Colonial times, Wellfleet was famous for its oysters and, in fact, was probably named for the renowned Wellfleet oyster beds of Blackwater Bay in England by early settlers from that region. Samuel de Champlain, visiting the area in 1606, called it Porte aux Huîtres and the Indians came from miles around to enjoy the shellfish bounty of the Wellfleet flats. For a century and a half after

The Cultivator

the Pilgrims came to Plymouth their descendants feasted on
bay oysters until in 1770 a mysterious disease decimated the
beds.

To counter this loss, the Wellfleet oystermen imported
seed from southern waters. Planted in the bay and left for
several years, they proved to have the same zesty flavor as
the original native oysters. During the entire nineteenth
century most of the oysters served throughout New
England came from these beds and it took forty schooners
with a capacity of 1750 bushels each to handle this lucrative
trade.

Then, about 1900, southern seed oysters became scarce,
partly because the fishermen left too few large oysters to
spawn, and partly through the removal for lime fertilizer of
large quantities of empty shells, which provide the best
surface for seed oysters to adhere to during their early life.

By the years just prior to World War I shipments had
fallen to 16,000 barrels a year but the *Cultivator* still planted
young Chesapeake Bay oysters in Wellfleet Bay and
dredged them up a few years later when they had acquired
the tang that made them favorites in the saloons and oyster
bars of Boston and New York.

May, June, July and August were slow months and
during most of this time the *Cultivator* remained tied up at
the Sealshipt Oyster Company pier near the Wellfleet
depot. But on the occasions of the C.C.C.C. excursions
she appeared at the Town Wharf festooned with pennants
and flying the American flag from her squat derrick mast.

Rows of canvas folding chairs filled her broad deck except
for the array of pots, pans, crates of food and tubs of
beverages clustered about the pilot house. When everyone
was aboard, a toot of her klaxon signaled "Cast off!" and her

throatily chugging engine sent her gliding out of the harbor.

Arrived in the Horseshoe, the harbor of Billingsgate Island, the passengers were rowed ashore in the *Cultivator's* dinghy and it took a dozen or more trips to ferry all hands plus the great heap of baggage and provender ashore.

Organization was the watchword. Division of labor had been carefully worked out between women and men, and everyone knew what was expected of him. Two or three men had the job of digging clams from the clean, sandy flats.

While they were thus engaged, other men erected a fly tent made from the mainsail of the former sloop *Ethel Young*. Still others dug a round, shallow pit about five feet in diameter in the sandy beach and lined it with rocks from the dilapidated jetty and the foundation stones of tumbled-down homes. Then they gathered great heaps of rockweed.

When they had finished their task, they heaped the pit high with driftwood and timbers from the old houses, poured kerosene over the wood and set it ablaze. Meanwhile, the women set to work wrapping pieces of fish, chicken and frankfurts in cheesecloth while others fell to peeling onions and potatoes, slicing salt pork and chopping quahaugs which Mr. Hopkins and the club president, Eddie Baker, opened on the spot.

Within a short time a savory aroma of frying salt pork and onions arose in clouds of steam from a high, black iron kettle suspended over a blazing fire built on the beach. The clam chowder that gave the club its name and its *raison d'être* was under way.

By now the initial preparations were finished, tent up, chairs set up, fires built, and when the clam diggers came straggling up the shore with their loaded buckets, it was time to go for a swim. Donning bathing suits in the privacy of the abandoned dwellings, all who wished plunged into the clean, sparkling waters of the Horseshoe.

The others sat on the beach or in the shade of the fly tent, chatting and enjoying the peaceful surroundings of sea and sky and sand. White sails flecked the blue bay, birds wheeled overhead and to the north a wisp of black smoke revealed the progress of the steamer *Dorothy Bradford* as she approached Provincetown Harbor on her run from Boston.

By the time the swimmers had dried themselves in the sun and dressed, the steaming contents of the iron kettle were ready to eat. At some appropriate moment practiced hands had added sliced potatoes and chopped quahaugs to the pot, and now, at the last instant, the expert cooks among the ladies—and that included practically all of them—gathered round the kettle, watching critically while one of their number added warm milk to the chowder, the final crucial step.

If the milk had ever curdled, the pourer would undoubtedly have dropped her ladle and perished on the spot—as well she might, for she could never have lived down her shame. But the milk never curdled and presently bowls of smoking hot quahaug chowder were being passed among the assemblage to the fervent tributes of the participants.

"Well," the chief architect of this ambrosial triumph would modestly reply, "I guess it's all right. Tastes kind of good, if I do say so."

Pilot biscuits were served with the chowder, not the namby-pamby pilot biscuits of today, but large, round affairs of a granitic consistency that enabled them to be preserved in a lifeboat cask for months on end. You almost had to soak them in order to chew them, but no chowder was considered complete without them.

The chowder represented a sort of early soup course, a temporary stop-gap until the *pièce de résistance* was ready. It took quite a while to prepare. After two hours, when the blazing driftwood and timbers in the pit had burned to white-hot embers, the coals were raked to the sides of the smoking pit. The fierce heat had blackened the white sand for several feet around and the sand had to be raked before one could approach the pit. A cup of water tossed on the rocks vanished in a crackling puff of steam.

Working quickly, Eddie Baker and his helpers spread a six-inch layer of rockweed over the smoldering stones, precipitating a huge cloud of steam. Onto this bed of rockweed went a bushel of steamer clams, on top of them three dozen of Cap'n Lombard's two-pound lobsters, three dozen pieces of Cap'n Davis's cut-up chicken, three dozen of Cap'n Lombard's fresh mackerel, three dozen of Mr. Wiley's frankfurts, three dozen assorted white and sweet potatoes and four dozen ears of Uncle Ben Eaton's sweet corn in their husks. Chicken, fish and frankfurts were all individually wrapped in cheesecloth.

The smoldering rocks around the edge of the pit were covered with rockweed and a canvas sail was stretched completely over the pit, held down by rocks and sand shoveled around the sides. Soon delectable odors rose in steam through the tightly stretched canvas.

During the hour that it took the contents of the pit bake to cook, Eddie Baker and Mr. Hopkins passed around cherry stones on the half-shell which they had saved out when opening the quahaugs for the chowder.

Opening the bake was a ritual. While everyone gathered

in a circle around the pit, Eddie Baker knelt beside it, long-handled fork in hand. Brushing away the sand, he would cautiously raise a small fold of canvas and peer underneath it through the steam. Then in would go the fork, out would come a lobster, to the cheers of the onlookers.

"Well," Eddie would say, "don't look's if he's going to crawl far. I guess the bake's done."

For the next hour or so, no sounds were heard save for the cracking of lobster shells, the husking of corn and a contented murmur of desultory conversation. I recently read a magazine article which purported to instruct the reader in the mechanics of putting together a clam bake—in a pressure cooker yet, God save the mark! It suggested a half-dozen clams as a typical individual portion. Had any self-respecting C.C.C.C.C. member been served a half-dozen clams he would have been outraged. And if any member had stopped at a half-dozen clams, he would have been stripped of his insignia on the spot. Indeed, it was not for nothing that Father was elected Vice President of the C.C.C.C. on the day he was still eating clams when they pulled the tent down on him.

The meal ended with hot coffee or ice-cold soda and watermelon and then, not surprisingly, the adult club members sat or lay quietly on the beach. For the younger element, however, it was a time to explore the ruins of the old houses, to climb the iron framework of Billingsgate Light tower, to hunt for shells across the flats and perhaps to tuck away one more soda before it was time to pack up the baggage and board the *Cultivator* for the sail home across the sunset-tinted waters of the bay.

After the Mail

ALTHOUGH the old Cape offered plenty of activities during the daylight hours, it was when the kerosene lights came on that things really started to swing. And sway. The difficulty for the visitor lay in choosing among the various opportunities that presented themselves.

Most of these opportunities, however, were dependent upon the arrival of the evening train from Boston which brought people, mail, movie films, orchestras, newspapers and other items necessary for the pursuit of social undertakings. As a result, the average evening began with the ritual known as "going for the mail."

The mail train arrived at Wellfleet at 8:00 P.M. Twenty minutes or so before a smudge of black smoke over Blackfish Creek heralded its approach, villagers and summer visitors began to converge upon the local post office—men, women and children filling the small, bare lobby that smelled of ink and paper, and overflowing into the dusty street. Qu'augers and fishermen in faded denims mingled with shopkeepers and cottagers in business attire and flannels. Women in silks and flowered prints rubbed elbows with women in gingham and draped with shawls—all waiting with an air of expectancy.

While they waited, they conversed animatedly on all subjects under the sun—the increasing cost of living: "I say the country's going to hell in a basket when you got to pay twenty-five cents for a measly pound of butter"—the misdeeds of Pancho Villa along the Mexican border: "If this Carranzo or whatever his name is can't lick Villa, then I figure it's time we stepped in and did the job ourselves"— the spate of mackerel off Truro: "By gorry, you could walk a mile across them mackerel's backs dry shod!"—the growing lead of the Boston Red Sox in the pennant race of the American League: "If they can beat Chicago they'll take the pennant and the Series, too"—President Wilson's latest warning to the Imperial German Government against the torpedoing of merchant ships carrying American passengers: "By God, if Teddy Roosevelt was in the White House he'd do somethin' besides talk!"—and the best recipe for quahaug pie: "I put just a touch of nutmeg in with the clams. Give's 'em a mite of flavor, I always say."

When one tired of listening to the snatches of conversation eddying on all sides, one could study the posters tacked to the post office wall.

WANTED: DEAD OR ALIVE

Bernard Salva, aged 32, wanted for armed robbery and murder. Height 5'9", weight 158 pounds. Brown hair, brown eyes. Scar on left cheek. Probably armed and considered dangerous. $100 reward for information leading to his apprehension.

And then, suddenly, a rustle of expectation swept through the crowd and conversations abruptly suspended as Monkey Baker wheeled up to the curb in his pick-up truck. Filled with a sense of his grave responsibilities, he leaped from the cab, grabbed up a sack of mail and dragged it across the sidewalk into the back room of the post office.

Conversations resumed during the interval while the shadowy figures of the postmistress and her assistant passed to and fro behind the ground-glass window and envelopes appeared in the glass-doored boxes.

Cape Cod mailboxes provided an index into one's standing in the community. Transients, by which was meant anyone staying in town less than two weeks, could secure call boxes. These boxes did not open and their renters had to call at the window for their mail. This was one step above General Delivery. Residents and Long-Term Summer Visitors were accorded the dignity of lock boxes, which enabled them to pick up their mail at any time when the post office was open.

The locks were of the combination variety, and not the least interesting part of going for the mail was the operation of these locks. Turn knob to S and pointer to 3, then turn knob to L and, presto, the box would open. This saved standing in line to wait while the postmistress handed out letters, packages and conversation.

"My, how you've grown, sonny. Here's a bundle from Providence. Towels, feels like. I see Uncle Henry is coming to visit you next week. How's his arthritis? Better, I hope."

When at last the window opened with a rattling flourish, the crowd pressed forward, some to form in line, others to open their boxes, briefly scan the mail and then saunter out into the lamplit dusk. Now the evening was officially launched.

The post office was a popular trysting place for the younger generation, as represented by my sister Doris. She and Cousin Alfred and I used to set out for the mail together, walking three abreast along the weed-bordered oyster shell road. But arrived at the post office, she would infiltrate the assemblage, shortly to appear inside the lobby engaged in animated conversation with the Andover boy. The Andover boy was tall and skinny with large ears and wore a big A on his pullover sweater—glamorous in a repulsive sort of way.

When it was time to leave the post office, Doris and the Andover boy were not to be seen—at least, not without some looking. By scouting around, Cousin Alfred and I would eventually find them, sauntering slowly arm in arm along the lower road.

The first night we followed a few paces behind them until the Andover boy gave us a dime apiece to get lost. We spent this windfall at Nye's Ice Cream Parlor and looked forward to a small but steady income through the summer. But then Doris blabbed to Mother and our coup was summarily squashed.

On Tuesdays, Thursdays and Saturdays the evening train brought film for the moving picture theater next door to the Congregational Church. It took a half-hour to get the film to the theater and set up in the projector, so the show didn't begin until after eight-thirty. When it finally did get under way, though, it was usually worth attending, not only for the screenplay itself, but also for the fringe benefits of atmosphere and local color.

The theater itself was small and smelled vaguely of apples. A few moths made it through the screens or the opened doors to flit about in the movie projector's beam and occasional mosquitoes added their presence to the proceedings, but no Paramount or Palace Theater audience was more receptive or enthusiastic than those who gathered here

three nights a week to watch the silent dramas unfold.

Nor were they entirely silent. The small fry, overrunning the front rows, made it a practice to read the subtitles aloud for better understanding or for the benefit of younger brothers and sisters, and their chorusing voices rose as a sort of counterpoint to the music provided by the pianist.

On ordinary nights when Tom Mix was playing in *The Terror* or Lillian Gish in *Blossoms*, the pianist was a maiden lady of uncertain age. She accompanied tender passages between the screen lovers with suitable soft, romantic music, marred only slightly by the fact that she couldn't see her notes very well in the dim shadows below the platform. But when the U. S. Cavalry galloped to the rescue of beleaguered pioneers surrounded by Indians or the hero raced the train to the crossing, she swept into the *William Tell Overture* with grim precision.

On special occasions, however, such as the performance of *Shipwrecked Among Cannibals*, she was superseded by a one-man band who came down from Brockton on the evening train. He was a most talented and unusual musician.

He sat sort of sidesaddle at the piano bench, turned so that his right foot was free to pedal a bass drum and cymbal combination. A horn was fastened at the proper height to a rack in front of him and thus he was able to play piano, bass drum, cymbals and horn simultaneously. Sometimes, at appropriate moments, he uttered blood-curdling screams or rebel yells to accompany the action on the screen.

When the cannibals climbed over the ship's rail to attack the unsuspecting crew and he let go with full orchestra, punctuated with shouts, groans and piercing whoops, the effect was truly startling. So startling, in fact, that during one performance it impelled the operator to call hoarsely from the projection booth, "Chris' sake, I can't hear to run the machine!" This was important, for the hand-cranked projector had to be heard as well as seen to be sure that all was well.

The show began with a typewritten card thrown on the screen requesting the LADIES to PLEASE REMOVE their HATS. The feature picture was usually preceded by a short newsreel depicting such events as President Wilson hurrying jerkily to address the Congress or a troop of soldiers marching in a kind of rapid-fire Charlie Chaplin gait along Fifth Avenue.

After the projectionist had wound the newsreel back onto its spool and threaded in a new roll of film, the feature began to unfold with a loud clicking sound soon overshadowed by the music of the female pianist or the one-man band. When one reel ended, the projectionist flashed a notice on the screen: Reel Two Will Follow Immediately.

Sometimes it did; on other occasions when the film wasn't threaded correctly or the projector became balky it might be a matter of ten minutes or more before the show continued. At such times all too audible, though muttered, imprecations from the booth caused the female pianist to plunge hastily into "The Blue Danube Waltz" or "Rustle of Spring."

Halfway through the feature a short intermission took place during which advertisements were projected upon the screen. "WILEY'S GROCERY. Where Your Satisfaction Is Our Concern. A full line of fancy groceries, fruits and vegetables for your enjoyment. A. Wiley, Prop." and "NYE'S SOUVENIR SHOP. All Sorts Of Interesting Souvenirs Of Cape Cod. Delicious Ice Cream, College Ices And Beverages. TRY NYE." "You'll Find What You Want At Atwood's Hardware Store." "Church Supper. Methodist Church July 10. Admission 30 cents."

You could also buy homemade candy during intermission. One of the selectmen went up to Boston and visited a movie theater there. When he returned home, he announced that in the big city you could buy candy and popcorn right in the theayter and why wouldn't that be a good idea here? The townsfolk thought it would be and the result was that for several years a group of ladies supplied fudge and penuche done up in paper napkins at ten cents a bag.

Saturday nights were the most festive of all, for besides the movies and the entertainments at Chequesset Inn, it was also dance night.

In the earlier years these took the form of hurdy-gurdy

dances at the Old Town Hall. An itinerant Italian, who spent the rest of the week tramping the Cape Cod highways with hurdy-gurdy and monkey, used to leave the monkey at home and bring his ornate instrument to the Town Hall on Saturday evenings where, for a dollar, he cranked it from eight until ten.

From its time-worn interior issued the popular tunes of the day—"Down Among the Sheltering Palms," "Moonlight Bay," "By the Sea" and various Strauss waltzes. Everyone attended these galas, residents and summer visitors of all ages, and while the elders sat conversing on the sidelines, the younger element circled the hall in time to the jerky rhythms. The youngest element, including Cousin Alfred and myself, played tag and hide-and-seek around the fringes of the gathering until such time as a square dance was called.

Then everyone joined in, and while the rollicking music of "Turkey in the Straw" and "Seeing Nellie Home" tumbled from the hurdy-gurdy, young and old lurched and swung and stamped through the measures of a Portland Fancy or Commodore Hull's Victory. Some of the older people who had been brought up on this kind of fare did little intricate steps of their own while they awaited their turn in the set.

The caller was a man named Sam Rich who was a qu'auger by day and he brought to his calling a certain *joie de vivre* that bordered on abandon. He was a large, beefy man with a voice that shook the hall and when he called a turn, it stayed called. In a subsequent, more effete age, square dance callers began using megaphones and today most resort to microphones to make themselves heard.

There were, of course, no microphones at that time, but there were speaking trumpets which captains and mates used to communicate with seamen furling the topgallant sails in a storm. Sam Rich eschewed these artificial aids to increased volume, confidently relying upon the vocal equipment with which nature had generously endowed him.

His delivery was free-wheeling and so were the verses he bellowed out to keep the dancers moving. Red-faced and perspiring, he kept time to the music with arms and legs and torso while he chanted at the top of his lungs.

> "Bunch the gals like scairy cattle,
>   Then stampede 'em right and left,
> Now swing 'em till their backbones rattle,
>   Swing 'em while you feel their heft."

("Harry, you're dancin' in the wrong set. Get back there with Sarah where you b'long.")

"Gents to one side, gals to t'other,
    Do-si-do an' stomp your feet,
Leave your gal and find another,
    Grab and swing her nice and neat.

Let the dance floor feel your leather,
    Circle right an' sashay back.
Do-si-do an' come together
    While you give your gal a smack."

At ten o'clock your parents took you home.

Later on, when cars had become more common and transportation was no longer a problem, the dances, minus the hurdy-gurdy, were moved to the Big Chief Pavilion located two miles outside the village on the road to South Wellfleet.

Eddie Baker, President of the C.C.C.C.C., built the Big Chief Pavilion with help from Uncle Ben Eaton, and for a number of years it was the scene of the weekly dances. It was a large, wooden structure with a railing around the dance floor, an inverted V roof overhead and a low platform to accommodate the orchestra. Rolled-up canvas screens could be lowered to cover the sides in inclement weather.

The admission charge was twenty-five cents for adults, ten cents for children and on Saturday nights the Pavilion was well filled with both. Orchestras ranged from local pick-up ensembles through college groups to itinerant professional bands, and some of them were amazingly good. Cousin Alfred and I, who came primarily to watch rather than to participate, particularly enjoyed the music of a black quintet, especially the drummer who bounced his sticks off the floor and tossed them to the ceiling in a frenzy of rhythmic abandon.

Doris, on the other hand, attended these affairs strictly in the interests of terpsichore. Sometimes she met the Andover boy at the Pavilion; other times we brought him with us in the Pope-Hartford. In either case, he and Doris would melt into the throng of circling dancers tirelessly performing fox-trots, one-steps, waltzes and tangos throughout the evening. The Andover boy was a swoopy type of dancer with an up-and-down arm motion that gave him somewhat the look of the Hopkins pump in action. Doris said he danced divinely.

It was at the Big Chief Pavilion that love came to Cousin Alfred. The catalyst who awoke the gentle passion in his heart was a rather scrawny damsel of thirteen with her red hair in bangs above her blue-eyed, freckled face. The first inkling I had of his defection was when I suddenly noticed that, instead of watching the supreme stick-flinging efforts of the black drummer, he was staring transfixed at this young lady's awkward gyrations in the arms of her father.

Cousin Alfred did not dare approach the object of his adoration that evening, but during the week it transpired that she and her parents were visiting her aunt, and, further, that Mrs. Hopkins knew her aunt! On the following Saturday night introductions were made that resulted in Cousin Alfred, red-faced and flustered, guiding the fair maiden, whose name was Ruth, about the dance floor in a determined fox-trot. The burgeoning romance was unfortunately nipped in the bud when she had to return to her home in Wakefield next day.

I, too, had my turns on the polished surface, but in my case, the activity was completely unpremeditated and entirely against my wishes. Friends whom Mother and Father had met at the Chequesset Inn came one Saturday night to the Big Chief Pavilion, bringing with them their daughter, Ella, a rather beefy girl with dark curls who wore braces on her teeth.

To my dismay, it was suggested by Mother that I dance with Ella, a proposal endorsed by her parents and also by Ella, who announced that she loved to dance. There was no escape. Feeling stricken and perspiring freely, I maneuvered her grimly along the fringes of the floor, counting audibly as we waltzed interminably to the strains of "I'm Forever Blowing Bubbles."

Some of the more adventurous—and mobile—patrons used to drive to Nye's Souvenir Shop for college ices at intermission, but most of the customers were content to settle for the cold soda sold on the premises and a walk out into the pines to observe the moon as it lifted above the wooded dunes. Ella and I forewent that romantic interlude.

Certain of the churches and civic organizations took advantage—in more ways than one—of the summer visitors' presence to schedule minstrel shows and dramatic productions. These were the forerunner of today's summer theater, and they were held in parish auditoriums, lodge halls, schools and any other suitable buildings that would offer them asylum. They proved to be brisk money-makers for their sponsors. Blackface minstrel shows, with their topical songs and jibes at prominent local citizens and summer residents, proved particularly popular.

"Mistuh Interlocurator?"

"Yes, Mr. Bones. What is it?"

"Does y'all know Mistuh Dan Hopkins?"

"Why, certainly I know Dan Hopkins. What about him?"

"Well, suh, th' other day he went into Ora Davis's market to buy a chicken . . ."

"To buy a chicken?"

"Yassuh, Mistuh Interlocutus, an' Ora say, 'I'm sorry, Dan, but I can't give you any more credit. Your bill is bigger now than it should be . . .' "

"And what did Dan say, Mr. Bones?"

"Dan say, 'I know that, Ora, an' if you'll make it out for what it really should be, I'll pay it.' "

(Clash of bones, jingling thump of tambourines and hearty laughter from the audience.)

"And now, ladies and gentlemen, Brother Sambo Nickerson will sing an end song—'Alexander's Ragtime Band.' "

The drama, too, leaned heavily on comedy, farces such as *Jilted, The Bird on Nellie's Hat* and *Second Honeymoon*, as well as operettas. Since there were never a sufficient number of local thespians to fill out the cast of these latter productions, summer visitors were warmly welcomed as participants. At one performance of *H.M.S. Pinafore*, Doris played the part of Buttercup and the Andover boy was a British tar.

Even Cousin Alfred and I were pressed into service as "Plucky Yankee Boys" in a Civil War melodrama called *Hearts of Blue*. We had a single line that went, "Hurrah for the red, white and blue!" and we gave it our all. During the course of the action, the Union general tripped over his sword and skinned his knee and an outsize explosion of gunpowder offstage singed the curtain. With unintentional candor, the *Cape Cod Item & Bee* pronounced it a "bang-up performance."

Less public but nonetheless memorable were the gatherings two or three times a week in Mr. Hopkins's barn.

Present at these sessions were a handful of qu'augers, fishermen and former deepwater skippers who came to eat clams, drink beer and tell stories. Meetings were informal, the group consisting of whoever happened to drop by, but there were seldom less than a half-dozen on hand on any evening, and sometimes the attendance grew to ten or more.

In the quiet dusk, by ones and twos they would saunter through the yard to take their places in the half-circle of chairs set up just inside the wide barn doorway.

"Evenin', Dan."

"Evenin', Ote—Oz. Heave anchor and sit a spell."

A Rhode Island brewer, who was a friend of Father's, used to send down each summer two large barrels filled with bottles of beer, ale and malt wine, each wrapped in corrugated paper, and two dozen or so of these bottles lay in a tub of ice behind the chairs, together with an opener tied on a string. Before sitting down, each new arrival would select a bottle of his favorite brew, holding the label to the dim light of dusk.

Mr. Hopkins sat at one end of the half-circle, a bucket of littlenecks at his feet and, as the chairs filled up, he would reach for his knife, thrust into a crack in the wall, and start to open clams, passing them to those present.

Cap'n Dill, Cap'n Lambert, Eddie Baker, Cap'n Ryder, Cap'n Paine, Mr. Hopkins, Father and Uncle Thomas Moore were regulars. Though Uncle Thomas had more right than any of the others to be called Cap'n—for in his earlier years he had skippered sailing vessels to the far corners of the world—he was always known as Uncle.

Although he had sailed past Highland Light literally

hundreds of times, he had never seen it from shore in all his seventy-four years until we took him on the twelve-mile trip to North Truro in the Pope-Hartford. On that occasion, although he was interested in the lighthouse and its operation, he was more concerned with the inept maneuvering, as he conceived it to be, of a bark a few miles offshore.

"Back staysails!" he roared in quarter-deck tones, standing on the high cliff and waving his arms. "Hard astarboard, you nincompoop landlubber, or you'll have her hard aground on the shoal!"

Uncle Thomas was strictly temperance and looked askance upon alcoholic beverages, but in his seventies he was beginning to feel the ravages of time and tide and Father persuaded him that a little malt wine would do more good to his physical being than harm to his soul. Having taken Father's advice, he found that he did not dislike this medication and, in fact, rather enjoyed it. He would go home with two or three bottles of malt wine wrapped in a newspaper and return a day or so later with the empties similarly concealed.

"I have to say, Doctor," he would report, "I haven't felt as chipper in years as I have since I've been taking this tonic."

Cousin Alfred and I were regulars, too, sitting quietly in the shadows off to the side and listening with wide open ears. Sometimes we were overlooked and managed to remain there until well past our bedtime, absorbing the ebb and flow of salt-encrusted conversation.

There was never any talk of the weather, of sports, politics or the news. Discourse adhered strictly to the sea and seafaring. Mr. Hopkins might be reminded of the February morning when, as a boy, he had awakened to see from his bedroom window the masts of a brig thrust up from the water off Jeremy's Point.

"I put the glass on 'em," he went on to relate, "and, by gorry, I could see six figures clinging to the rigging. I hollered for my father and he came and took a look. Then he sent me to spread the news while he went down to the shore to his boat.

"I ran down the street, banging on doors and shouting and pretty soon there was half a dozen men joined my father on the beach. They jumped into his boat and set out, though there was a strong breeze blowing and the temperature was below freezing.

"Well, sir, as they came close, they could see the men lashed to the rigging and every one of 'em was coated with ice. They came up under the brig's stern—the *Eagle*, she was, out of Boston—and when they'd made a line fast and boarded her, they found all six men frozen to death, stiff as iron statues. She'd foundered on the bar in the night and the rest of her crew had drowned."

That would recall to Cap'n Dill's mind the story of Cap'n Lew Cobb who skippered the coasting schooner *Adelaide* out of Provincetown.

"Too bad they didn't have Cap'n Lew along," Cap'n Dill opined. "They say he could always tell where he was at sea just by tasting the bottom when they hauled the sounding lead. He'd look at the sand or mud, taste it, and say, 'We're over Handkerchief Shoal.' Folks figured he was making it up, so to speak.

"One time, the story goes, some fellers in his crew

thought they'd play him a prank to sort of call his bluff. Afore they put to sea they greased a lead and dipped her in a pot of geraniums and hid her in the fo'c'sle. Then one foggy night when they were taking soundings, they brought out the lead, wet her a bit and handed her to the skipper.

"He looks at the dirt, tastes it and lets out a gasp. 'Jumpin' Jehosophat,' he roars, 'the ocean's washed clean over Cape Cod and we're right over Aunt Mary Ryder's garden.'"

Mr. Hopkins had devised an ingenious arrangement to take care of the beer saturation problem. A funnel, thrust through a hole in the floor, was connected to a rubber hose which led into the convenience in the woodshed next door. Relief was thus simple and convenient without ever leaving the barn.

As full darkness came on, pipes and cigars glowed through the shadows until Mr. Hopkins lighted a kerosene lantern and hung it to a convenient nail. If the mosquitoes bothered, as they often did, he would light a stick or two of citronella which added their pungent scent to those of tobacco and kerosene. And presently, Uncle Thomas Moore's surprisingly soft voice would fill in a lag in the conversation.

"Do you recollect Josh and Oren Snow? Well, I guess they was before your time. They were twin brothers, as like as two peas in a pod. Both were cap'ns of vessels out of Boston for an importing firm—Russell's it was.

"I was cabin boy aboard Cap'n Oren's vessel, *Southern Cross*, and one day in Pernambuco Harbor he ran afoul of the law. It was one of those trumped-up charges those fellers were always trying to pull off in those days. Cap'n Oren was straight as a string and wouldn't have touched a penny

that didn't belong to him, but they brought this charge of
smuggling and they were going to fine him and maybe take
his vessel. Anyway, he knew he'd rot for months in prison
at the least.

"Well, it just so chanced that that night who should sail
into the harbor but Cap'n Oren's twin brother, Cap'n Josh.
Soon as he anchored, Cap'n Josh lowered a boat and came
over to see his brother aboard the *Southern Cross.* Cap'n
Oren told his brother how he was facing arrest and the two
of 'em rigged a plan.

"Next day, sure enough, we saw a cutter coming out
from shore full of policemen all dressed up in red and gold
braid. They came aboard us with a warrant for Cap'n
Oren's arrest.

" 'You'll find him aft,' the mate says.

"So aft the procession went and there on the quarter-deck
stood Cap'n Oren and Cap'n Josh, side by side, looking so
much alike that even I could hardly tell 'em apart.

" 'We have a warrant for the arrest of Cap'n Oren
Snow!' the leader of the policemen says.

" 'All right,' Cap'n Oren tells them, 'take him. But let me
warn you, gentlemen, that if you pick the wrong man,
you'll answer to the United States Government!'

"Well, the policemen looked at the two of 'em and fell to
jabbering among themselves and pretty soon off they went
and got into their boat and sailed ashore. And that was the
end of their plaguing Cap'n Oren."

Eddie Baker was not a seafaring man but he usually had a
story to tell. One that I recall concerned a goose-hunting
exploit on the Barnstable marshes.

"I was sort of caretaker at a camp there," Eddie said, "and

one fall night I was there alone. Long about five o'clock I woke up and I could hear a goose gabbling down by the creek. I figured it must have pitched in the evening before and was feeding before it flew off south.

"Well, I stood it long's I could and then says I, 'I'll just sneak down and collect that bird 'fore he gets away.' I didn't take much time. I pulled on a pair of pants over my nightshirt, shoved on my boots, grabbed my gun and off I went.

"I pussyfooted along slow and easy and the goose kept talking. Time I reached the creek it was getting light and, all at once, I could see the goose sitting in a little cove. I knew if I tried to get nearer he'd see me and fly and he was a long shot away. Time I got to shoot he'd be out of range so I figures to myself, 'I guess I'll take him right where he sits.'

"I poked my gun through the reeds, took a good bead and let fly. And, pow, that goose flopped over without even kicking. I jumped up and ran over to grab him and, by gorry, danged if he wasn't a live decoy tethered to an anchor on the bottom!

"Just about then I noticed a portly man running toward me, waving a shotgun. And who do you suppose it turned out to be?" Eddie paused for effect and glanced about. "Grover Cleveland, President of the United States!"

After a trenchant silence, Cap'n Paine asked, "What'd you say, Eddie?"

"I said," Eddie replied, " 'Mr. President, this is a hell of a spot for a Republican!' "

Breeches Buoys,
Bayberries & Submarines

ONE ACTIVITY we shared in common with present-day visitors to Cape Cod was that of sightseeing, and many of the places we discovered in our explorations in those early years became the scenes of annual pilgrimages. Some of them have disappeared completely, others remain today, attracting hordes of tourists, but these, too, have felt the changing touch of time.

One of our favorite excursions was the three-mile trip through scrub oak and pine to the Cahoon's Hollow Life Saving Station located on the outer beach at Wellfleet. In those days there were similar stations spaced at eight-mile intervals from Race Point near Provincetown all the way to Monomoy and Cape Cod Canal. But Cahoon's Hollow was the one we knew best.

Since the road to the station had been surfaced with ground-up oyster shells and the brush had been trimmed along its sides, it could be negotiated by the Pope-Hartford. As one neared the ocean, scrub oak and pine gave way to stunted trees no bigger than shrubs, and to a carpet of beach grass and hog cranberries. And then, topping a gentle rise, one came in sight of the station, huddled in a sandy hollow to protect it from winter storms.

Here at the top of the rise it was necessary to leave the car, for the slope to the station was deep sand. On one of our first visits Father attempted to drive closer and it took

Cahoon's Hollow Life Saving Station

the best efforts of Neptune, the station horse, to drag us out
of this predicament.

As you waded through the soft sand, you could catch a
vista of blue sea between two dunes and, perched at the top
of the right-hand one, the little, weathered lookout hut
which was manned twenty-four hours a day. Arrived at the
wide screen door of the station, you knocked and then
walked into the day room, gay with red-and-white checked
curtains at the windows and with framed ship pictures
around the walls.

In so doing, you entered into a strange new world, a
world of spit and polish, of shining woodwork and gleaming
brass. The first floor of the building consisted of the large
day room, a kitchen and a well-filled apparatus room. The
crew of eight slept in a dormitory on the second floor which
also provided beds for shipwrecked sailors rescued from the
sea.

The crew was always happy to welcome visitors. There were no radios, no television sets, the newspapers arrived only sporadically and the main contact of these lonely men with the outside world came from the occasional visitor who knocked at their door.

Since the crew partook of five hearty meals a day, it was almost impossible to arrive when they were not eating or preparing to eat. But this was no problem, for they always seemed to have plenty of food on hand and to be hurt if one refused to join them.

Sometimes, when we had eaten a picnic lunch on the shore of Long Pond on our way to Cahoon's Hollow, it was something of a struggle to sit down to a platter of hamburgers an inch thick and as big around as tea plates, country fried potatoes, slabs of homemade bread and wedges of hot apple pie. But Cousin Alfred and I, especially, were always ready to fight satiety in the interests of etiquette. Doris, on the other hand, who was dieting, often contented herself with only one piece of pie.

They were good cooks, those old-time life savers. Each man took his turn in the kitchen and each man had his specialty. The Number One man, or mate, specialized in pies; in one of Mother's old cookbooks there is a recipe in her handwriting entitled "Tom Wood's Apple Pie." He gave her the recipe one Sunday afternoon and it was intriguing to hear this brawny six-foot man, built on the lines of a heavyweight prizefighter, disclosing his culinary secrets.

"I always use a fork to mix the dough together, Ma'am, and I try to keep everything cold. You want to cut the shortenin' into your flour with two knives. Cut it up fine so's the lumps is about the size of peas. And I find just a pinch of sal'ratus makes your crust nice an' light."

Next to eating with the crew, we enjoyed hearing their tales of the wrecks that had occurred during the winter. Scarcely a season went by that didn't see some luckless vessel come to grief on the offshore bars. Hearing about them firsthand from the men who had fought to save their crews was the next best thing to having been an eyewitness to the event.

Sometimes their fights were desperate ones. There was the Italian bark *Castagna*, bound from Montevideo to Weymouth, Massachusetts, with a cargo of cattle horns. On the night of February 17, 1914, as she approached Cape Cod, a tremendous gale blasted out of the northeast. Mountainous waves battered the staggering ship and fierce winds tore her sails.

Toward midnight, despite their efforts to beat offshore, the crew heard the ominous roar of breakers. The skipper, Captain Giuseppe Gavi, ordered a stern anchor thrown overboard, but the anchor dragged and early in the morning the *Castagna* crashed onto a bar. After sending up rockets, crew and captain sought refuge by climbing into the rigging.

The rockets were seen from shore and the Cahoon's Hollow crew prepared to go to the stricken ship's assistance. They knew that the sailors would be too numb to handle the breeches buoy lines, so they attempted the only other alternative: launching a lifeboat through the surf.

The life-saving service, now the U.S. Coast Guard, has an unofficial motto: *You have to go out, but you don't have to come back.* And so the Cahoon's Hollow crew went out.

The first time, their boat was swept ashore. The second time they fought their way beyond the breakers and crept toward the bark. But they were too late. One after another, the Captain and four sailors lost their grip on the rigging and dropped into the raging seas.

When the Cahoon's Hollow men reached the ship, eight men were left aboard, along with a yellow cat and a parrot which the life savers brought ashore. The *Castagna* was the last square-rigged vessel to leave her bones in the Cape Cod sands. Today I have a miniature life preserver with a pair of oars and a boathook fashioned from a timber of the ill-fated bark. It was given to Father by Captain Tobin, keeper of the Cahoon's Hollow station.

Best of all, when the talk had run its course, was a visit to the gleaming apparatus room. This contained two lifeboats, each 24 feet long and 8 feet wide. Each carried six rowing oars and a steering oar, along with life jackets and boat hooks. Air tanks at bow and stern gave the boats additional buoyancy, and righting lines running along the sides below the cork fenders enabled the boats to be turned right side up if they capsized in the surf. The boats were mounted on cradles with wide, grooved metal wheels.

Close beside them rested the beach cart, equipped with a large reel of heavy rope and several boxes of smaller shot lines. A breeches buoy and tackle lay atop the boxes, partially hiding the canvas-covered Lyle gun. Buckets, axes, shovels, lanterns and brass speaking-trumpets were fastened securely to the cart's sides. On the walls of the room hung Coston lights, signal flags and a large first aid chest.

One could spend an hour or more inspecting this spotless equipment and Cousin Alfred and I often did. After several visits we knew exactly how each piece was used, but still we liked to have Frank Rice accompany us on our tours and tell us about the various pieces of apparatus. Frank was our favorite life saver and his somewhat unusual locutions only made his conversation the more fascinating.

"Which boat went out to the *Castagna*?" we asked him that next summer.

"We took this one, we did," he replied, laying a hand on its gunwale.

"Were you in it, Frank?"

"Yes. I sat here, I did, and terrible rough it was. We like to capsize, we like, and as we came near we could see the men hangin' in the riggin', we could."

"What did you do when you got there?"

"Well, we went aboard, we did, an' lugged the crew into our boat, along with the cat and parrot. An' the Old Man says, 'Let's get out of here' and we come in, we did."

He told us about the parrot. "Used to cuss terrible, he did. It was in Eyetalian, but you could tell it was cussin', you could."

If you went to Cahoon's Hollow on certain days of the week you could see the life savers drilling with the apparatus and if you were fortunate you could even take part in the activities. But on Tuesday mornings the crew practiced launching the lifeboat, and in this exercise you remained strictly an observer.

When Captain Tobin gave the command, two men flung open the wide outside doors of the apparatus room while others pushed one of the boats down the ramp. At the same time, Joe Young, who was Number Three, came up leading Neptune from the nearby stable.

As soon as they had the horse hitched to the cradle, Joe

led him to the beach through the soft sand with the rest of
the men pushing at the boat's stern. When they got to the
shore they'd unhitch the horse and lift the boat to the edge
of the surf, bow to sea.

Each man took his place beside the thwart from which he
would row. Tom Wood, the Number One man, was the
stroke and he sat with Henry Eaton in the bow. Captain
Tobin steered from the stern with the long oar. He gave the
command to launch, too.

The largest waves come in groups of three and after the
third wave there's a patch of slack water that the life savers
called a slatch. This is followed by a backwash toward the
sea and the crews always tried to launch in the slatch so the
undertow would help float the boat.

Captain Tobin would watch for the slatch and then,
"Now!" he'd roar and the crew would shove off, each man
climbing in and grabbing his oar as his section of the boat
floated free. Last of all, Captain Tobin would jump in over
the stern and pick up his steering oar.

Sometimes, when the surf was heavy, the boat would
broach and sweep ashore or else a breaker would crash over
the bow and fill the boat half full of water. Even in their
boots, oilskins and lifejackets the men would be soaked. I
often thought how much worse it must be on a winter's
night with snow, sleet and bitter wind adding to the
torment of icy seas, but these soakings never seemed to
harm them.

"If you let salt water dry on you," Frank Rice told us,
"you'll never catch cold, you won't."

Breeches buoy drill on Thursday morning was something
else. Cousin Alfred and I liked to be on hand for that two or

three times a summer because the crew was always glad to have someone take the part of a shipwrecked sailor and ride the breeches buoy.

They used the flagpole, which, with its horizontal spar, was the mast and spar of a sailing ship, for the breeches buoy drill. Thursday mornings when Captain Tobin ordered, "Action!" the crew would haul the beach cart from the apparatus room to a point a hundred and fifty yards or so from the mast.

Two men pulled the heavy sand anchor from the cart. This consisted of two six-foot two-by-fours bolted together to form a cross. In its center there was an iron ring called a bull's-eye. The anchor was buried in the sand with only the bull's-eye showing. Meanwhile, other men set up a tall wooden crotch in front of the anchor and tied a hawser from it to the bull's-eye.

At this time one crew member brought up a wooden chest containing the shot line. The chest was three feet square and the top and sides came off in one piece, revealing 500 yards of linen line wound in layers around wooden pegs. The life savers called it a faking box. When the pegs were removed, the line was ready to be shot.

While these preparations were being made, Captain Tobin was giving his attention to the Lyle gun set up beside the faking box. First he loaded the gun with a gunpowder cartridge. Then he thrust a steel projectile down the short barrel. The ring in the end of the projectile's shaft stuck out of the muzzle and to this ring Captain Tobin tied one end of the shot line, after wetting it so the powder wouldn't burn it.

When all was ready, the Captain aimed the gun over the

mast and yanked the lanyard. A dull boom echoed down the beach, a puff of black smoke burst from the muzzle and the projectile soared away, pulling the line behind it. The projectile carried several hundred yards but the line dropped over the spar. That was where Cousin Alfred and I came in.

"Now," Captain Tobin would inquire gruffly, "do we have any volunteers for the breeches buoy?"

Before the words were out of his mouth, Cousin Alfred and I were halfway to the mast. Swarming up to the spar, we waited eagerly for the next step in the drama to unfold.

The next step was that the crew attached the shot line to a pulley fastened to a whip line—an endless loop of rope reeled on the beach cart. Now by hauling on our end of the shot line Cousin Alfred and I could pull the whip line out to our perch on the spar. Fastened to it was a piece of black wood called a tally board.

Printed in white on each side were instructions telling shipwrecked mariners how to proceed. One side was in English, the other in French, but Cousin Alfred and I didn't need either of these languages. From long practice we hitched the whip line pulley to the mast and then waved our arms in signal to the "shore."

Now the hawser came jerking out to the mast as the crew hauled on the whip line. This, too, carried a tally board telling us to make fast the hawser to the mast above the pulley. When this was done we signalled again and the great moment was at hand. Now the crew hung the breeches buoy and a pulley to the whip line at their end of the hawser. The breeches buoy was a cork life ring with a pair of short canvas breeches fastened to it. Now when the life savers hauled on the whip line the breeches buoy came swinging along the hawser to the spar.

By dint of age Cousin Alfred took the first ride and it was a little scary to be left alone, clinging to the spar sixty feet above the ground, watching as my companion rode grandly from mast to beach. It was scary, too, when the breeches buoy came back to insert one's legs into the short trousers while still trying to hang onto the spar. But at last the transfer was made and, clutching the ring in both hands, I rode triumphantly to the beach, filled with a sense of my importance.

No trip to Cahoon's Hollow was complete without a visit to the little lookout hut perched on top of a dune overlooking the ocean. The shingled hut had windows on three sides and was furnished with a tiny stove, a chair and a chart showing the smokestack designs and house flags of various steamship lines.

A big spyglass rested across two pegs below the front window with a pair of binoculars hanging beside it. On the front wall hung wooden discs with holes bored around their edges. The discs were marked Schooner, Brig, Bark, Sloop, Steamer and so on, a disc for each type of vessel that passed by. As soon as a ship came in view the life saver on duty in the hut would identify its type and place a peg in the appropriate disc. This way they kept track of all the passing shipping.

It was fun to sit in the hut watching the procession of coastal vessels. There were a lot of them in those days, the majority of them sailing vessels—schooners, barks, brigs and sloops, along with strings of coal barges towed by puffing tugs, steamers leaving a plume of black smoke along the horizon and occasional naval vessels bound for Provincetown. Cousin Alfred and I vied with one another to identify the various craft, our arguments moderated by whoever was on duty at the time.

"What's that vessel, boys?" the lookout man would ask.

"It's a bark."

"No, it isn't. It's a barkentine."

"It is not! It's a bark! I'll bet you a nickel!"

"Well . . . all right. I'll bet you. Who's right, Joe?"

"Neither of you. It's a brigantine. See her for'ard mast, square-rigged, and her mainmast is rigged fore-and-aft. Barks and barkentines have three masts."

In time we learned the intricacies of sailing vessel rigs and could even tell a yawl from a ketch. This knowledge was extremely important to me at the time, for I had every intention of becoming a life saver as soon as I had attained sufficient years. There was no mistaking the white steamers of the United Fruit Company on their way to and from the Islands and Central American ports.

From the hut you could see not only the ships that passed before your eyes, but also the graves of ships that had been wrecked here many years ago. Looking out over the calm ocean you could see the shoals, pale green against the dark blue of deep water.

"Yonder lies the *Whidah*," the lookout would tell us, pointing, "the pirate Bellamy's ship. She went down in 1717 and all but two of her hundred and forty men with her. You can sometimes see her caboose at low water."

The British frigate *Somerset* sank here in 1798 with a loss of seventy men and, to the north, the ship *Jason* foundered in 1893 with the loss of all her crew save one. Captain Tobin was the last man to see the steamer *Portland* as she disappeared into the snowy darkness on the night of November 27, 1898.

Each member of the Cahoon's Hollow crew spent four hours on duty in the lookout hut and then, when his relief had appeared, he took his turn at patrolling the beach, hiking four miles up or down the shore to a shack located halfway to the next station. Here he exchanged brass tags with the patrolman from the neighboring station and then plodded four miles back through the soft sand. Thus, every mile of beach from Provincetown to the end of Monomoy was covered day and night.

This eight-mile hike wasn't so bad on an August afternoon but it could be sheer misery on a January night with a northeaster driving snow and icy spray across the beach. At night the men carried lanterns and Coston lights hung from their belts. The Coston light contained a red fire cartridge in a metal holder and when you struck a plunger

in the handle it ignited the cartridge and sent up a lurid crimson flare. If the patrolman saw a ship too close to shore, he would warn it off with the light. Or, if a ship was already aground, the flare told her crew that help was coming.

Today the sailing vessels are gone and most of the coastal shipping. And with their passing the old stations have been phased out, too. Today only four remain—one at Race Point, another at Chatham, a third at Woods Hole and the fourth at Sandwich. But these have changed completely. Amphibious craft, diesel-powered lifeboats, radio telephones and helicopters have taken the place of horses, oars and Coston lights. But, to me, the shades of Captain Tobin and his Cahoon's Hollow life-saving crew still wander the sands of the outer beach.

Something akin to the trips we made to the Hollow were our visits to the lighthouses that guarded the curving coast. Our favorite was Cape Cod or Highland Light at Truro, perhaps because it was the most powerful or, perhaps, because of the souvenir shop next door which sold ice cream and candy, as well as all sorts of fascinating mementos of the light.

Highland Light was a popular tourist mecca and sometimes there would be as many as twelve persons waiting in line for a chance to ascend the tower. This was about as many as the small, round chamber in which the light was located could accommodate so you had to wait until the preceding party had finished its tour.

When your turn came, you followed the keeper along a narrow corridor into the tower and then began to climb the spiral metal stairs that led to the lantern. As you circled your way upward you could see a heavy weight suspended through the ceiling high above. Linked to gears, the weight dropped slowly, causing the light to revolve and making the tower into a sort of giant grandfather's clock. The mechanism had to be rewound three times a night.

The stairs ended at a trapdoor through which you emerged into a small, circular room (the lantern) almost completely filled by the light. While you waited for the last member of your party to climb through the trapdoor and take his place beside the light, you had an opportunity to inspect your surroundings.

The circular walls of the lantern were made of heavy glass, interspersed with metal strips and curtained halfway to the ceiling. In front of you the four-sided lens rested on a huge metal drum. A short iron ladder led into the lens itself, which was large enough for a man to stand up in. A Welsbach mantle sat on a small pedestal inside the lens which also contained a U-shaped vaporizer to feed the mantle.

The tower and its lantern was as neat and spotless as Cahoon's Hollow Life Saving Station and it smelled of metal polish and the kerosene which at that time fueled the light.

When all members of the group were present and accounted for, the keeper would begin his spiel and, although the keepers changed from time to time, their words almost never did. I often suspected that they learned their speeches by rote from the book of Lighthouse Regulations. Cousin Alfred and I could recite their talks almost word for word.

"Ladies and gentlemen," the keeper would announce,

"you are now looking at the second most powerful light on the Atlantic Coast, the most powerful being at Navasink, New Jersey. The first lighthouse was built upon this site in 1798. The present tower was built in 1857 and is sixty-six feet tall. Since the cliff here rises one hundred and seventeen feet, the light itself is one hundred and eighty-three feet above the ocean.

"The present light was installed in 1901 and the bull's-eye lenses were made in France at a cost of fifty thousand dollars. The light, which weighs one ton, is afloat upon a bed of mercury and is so delicately balanced that, as you see, I can turn it by the pressure of my finger.

"The lamp develops 192,000 candlepower which the bull's-eye lenses increase to half a million candlepower . . . son, please stop turning the light . . . and it can be seen thirty-five miles at sea on a clear night. It flashes a white light every six seconds, the light being revolved by a clockwork mechanism.

"You will note that the windows are curtained during the day. If this were not done, the sun's rays reflecting from the prisms, like a giant burning glass, would set fire to Provincetown."

Most keepers finished their talks by inviting those who wished to do so to climb the short ladder, one at a time, into the lens, the better to inspect the gleaming prisms and the mechanism. One keeper had cause to regret his offer when a stout lady whose enthusiasm surpassed her judgment accepted his invitation. We were not present upon this occasion, but the keeper told us about it later.

The lady, it seems, was somehow able to thrust her ample proportions through the lens entrance but when she had completed her inspection and was ready to descend, the heaviest part of her became firmly wedged in the opening.

"We got ahold of her limbs," the keeper said, "and we hauled and we tugged but it seemed like she only stuck tighter. I was cussed if I knew what to do. We couldn't cut away the metal flooring which is gov'ment property, anyway, and we couldn't cut away the woman, so b'god—pardon the expression, ma'am—I figured maybe she was going to have to stay there till she starved down thin enough to get out."

The mental image of the unfortunate woman revolving slowly through the night was intriguing to contemplate.

"Well, finally I recollected I had a pail of axle grease in the shed so I went down and fetched it up. By now the lady wanted out any way she could get out so she said to do whatever we wanted to just so's she got loose.

"We daubed her up pretty good and got as much grease as we could around the opening. Then when we got her fair set for launching, we got a good hold on her and hauled away. And, by gorry, she popped through that hole as slick as a whistle. But I'll tell you," he added, shaking his head, "ever since then I size up the crowd pretty good before I invite 'em to go up in the lens."

After inspecting the light, you could go through a door onto a balcony. From this spot 183 feet above the sea the view was spectacular. On the ocean side you could look out upon a vast blue expanse, dotted by the white sails of coasting vessels. Sometimes there would be a dozen in view at once. In the opposite direction one had a birdseye view of the houses of Provincetown with the gray shaft of the Pilgrim Monument rising above them. On a clear day you could see the hills of Manomet across the bay and follow the circling shoreline of Cape Cod all the way to the Canal.

Since then the light has been electrified and its intensity increased to four million candlepower, visible forty-five miles at sea. But today the souvenir shop is gone and a wire fence puts the lighthouse off limits to visitors.

Trips to Provincetown were always welcome features of Cape Cod summers and were undertaken mostly for pleasure, but also partly for more utilitarian considerations.

For one thing, Provincetown was the nearest point where one could get the Pope-Hartford washed. Its ablutions took place four or five times a summer in Paige's Garage on Commercial Street. The garage sat on fill above the sandy beach and its rear door provided an excellent spot from which to watch the activities of the busy harbor. Paige's Garage also ran a fleet of open sightseeing buses in which you could explore the town or take short trips to Race Point and Highland Light.

For another thing, Provincetown was the nearest community to boast a drug store. To be sure, you could buy Lydia Pinkham Compound, Dr. Sloane's Stomach Pills and Bishop's Elixir at Nye's Souvenir Shop, but for prescription medicines you had to visit the Adams Pharmacy in Provincetown.

Thus, in time of need, Father would approach this emporium, prescription pad in hand, and while we waited for the pharmacist to supply the medicine, we would enjoy an ice cream soda or a college ice.

In those days, druggists didn't pour ready-made precription pills from a large container into small containers or decant liquids from jugs into plastic flasks. Instead, the pharmacist had row upon row of apothecary jars, all neatly labeled, reposing on his back room shelves. From these he would select the proper ingredients which he then proceeded to mix with mortar and pestle.

At least, we always hoped he would select the correct ingredients. When a jar was empty, he had a habit of crossing the name on the label off with a pen and then adding in his own handwriting the name of the materia medica with which he had replaced the jar's original contents. Sometimes he did this several times so that a jar might be labeled: ~~Bismuth~~, ~~Potassium~~, Arsenic. At first, Father kept a wary eye on the pharmacist's concoctions but he soon learned that his system, though unusual, was seemingly foolproof and that he could lay his hand on the proper container almost without looking—which sometimes he didn't.

Most of our time in Provincetown, however, was spent in exploring the main street and the narrow, hollyhock-bordered lanes, visiting old but ever-new points of interest. Provincetown was a rare spot in those days, an unexploited, unabashed fishing village, just beginning to be discovered by a group of writers and artists who later became famous—Eugene O'Neill, John Whorf, Susan Glaspell and Wilbur Daniel Steele among them. The entire town had a rich, bracing aroma of fish, mingled with the scent of roses, pinks and hydrangeas and, in those uncrowded years, you could walk in the streets with impunity.

Near the top of the list of things-to-do in Provincetown was the ascent of the Pilgrim Monument. The granite tower, 252 feet tall, stands upon a 100-foot elevation, so that a person at the top looks out from a height of 352 feet above the harbor.

It was completed in 1910 at a cost of $100,000 and its Renaissance design was copied from the Torre del Mangia in Siena, Italy. The incongruity of erecting an Italian tower in a Yankee fishing village to honor a band of emigrant Englishmen apparently troubled no one, certainly not Cousin Alfred and me as we raced one another up the inclined planes that lead to the grilled walkway at the top.

From this pinnacle one had an even grander prospect than from Highland Light. Below sprawled the clustered houses of the village and the several wharves extending into the bustling harbor. Small craft scuttled like water beetles in and out among the anchored shipping and the sleek gray Navy vessels moored offshore.

Beyond Wood End and Race Point the ocean stretched to curved horizons, carrying on its wrinkled surface the sails of coasting vessels. Your eye could follow the entire sweep of the Cape and sometimes you could see the Myles Standish Monument at Duxbury across Cape Cod Bay.

When you glimpsed a white dot on the horizon, trailing a plume of black smoke behind it, it was time to run down the ramps of the monument and to make your way to Steamship Wharf, for the white dot was the steamer *Dorothy Bradford* approaching Provincetown on its daily trip from Boston.

En route you had time to visit a couple of souvenir shops and perhaps, if affluent, to purchase a felt pen wiper with Souvenir of Provincetown embroidered upon it, or a watch fob bearing a likeness of the Pilgrim Monument. The Provincetown shops carried an even larger stock and a wider assortment of goods than Nye's Souvenir Shop in Wellfleet, and the displays of crockery, glass, leather, pennants, pillows, ash trays, lamps, vases, shells and wooden artifacts were fabulous beyond belief.

By the time you had exhausted your curiosity, or at least your modest allowance, in the Provincetown gift shops, the *Dorothy Bradford* would be rounding Wood End, her whistle hoarsely saluting the harbor shipping. At the sound, practically everyone in town flocked to the wharf to meet her.

Walking along the wharf and peering over its edge, you could see the rippling water shade to green and then to blue as it deepened, its shimmering beauty in no whit detracted from by the occasional pieces of watermelon rind or the more than occasional dead fish floating belly upward on its surface.

There were no harbor sightseeing craft or speedboat rides

Dorothy Bradford

in those days, no party boats or charter fishing boats. The only craft tied up to the wharf were Navy longboats, fishing vessels and an occasional lumber schooner. Piles of logs lay heaped along the dock beside the railroad tracks, waiting to be loaded aboard freight cars standing on the siding.

Often, as you made your way toward the pier's end, you would pass by a fishing smack unloading cod and haddock from Georges Banks or Newfoundland. Men in rubber knee boots pitchforked fish into baskets which were hauled to the dock and dumped in silvery cascades on the flooring.

Each day when the steamer arrived two or three dory loads of half-naked Portuguese youngsters materialized out of nowhere to dive for coins which the tourists tossed into the water.

The end of the pier was where the action was, however, for it was here that the crowd gathered to watch the *Dorothy Bradford* being warped into her berth. Passengers lining the rail waved hats and handkerchiefs to welcomers on the dock and shouted conversations mingled with the throaty blasts of the steamer's whistle. Hawsers fell clumping to the dock to be seized and hung around the capstans and with a final hoot and a jangle of bells the ship came to rest.

To me, though, this vessel was not the *Dorothy Bradford*, just in from Boston. She was the S. S. *Mauritania*, docking in triumph after her record-breaking crossing from Queenstown. And the women in wide hats and veils, carrying parasols, and the men in cloth caps and Panamas, nonchalantly descending the gangplank, were to me world travelers from distant lands. Assorted uncles, aunts and cousins came occasionally on the *Dorothy Bradford* to visit us and it gave me a great sense of pride to step forward and claim kinship with these sophisticated cosmopolites.

During the three hours or so that the steamer remained in port, streets and shops became more crowded but the traffic was almost entirely pedestrian, save for Paige's sightseeing buses inching their way with honking horns along Commercial Street. During a part of the summer the throngs were swelled by sailors from the naval vessels in the harbor. Then tough marines of the shore patrol stood on corners, ready for any emergency.

But there was little trouble. Aside from their baseball rivalry, townspeople and sailors got along well together. The sailors played tag atop the Pilgrim Monument and baseball in their field behind the town. And when the fleet left, almost everyone was sorry to see it go.

Today there are several candle factories on Cape Cod, turning out thousands of items from slim tapers to ornate giants a foot tall and five inches in diameter. But in the early days there was only one that we knew of. This factory was located at North Truro and consisted of a single room where a stout woman sat at a bench, dipping wicks into a pot of melted bayberry wax. She had a younger and slimmer assistant whose duty it was to box the finished candles.

We used to visit this manufactory once or twice a summer, both to lay in a supply of candles and also to watch the dexterity of the stout woman in the various steps of their fabrication. Her tools and methods were simple in the extreme.

The rectangular vat containing the melted wax rested on a sort of brazier which kept its contents hot. In her hands the woman held a slim, foot-long steel rod to which eight-inch lengths of candle wicking were tied at two-inch intervals.

Each time she dipped the wicks into the hot wax, a coating adhered to them. Having dipped one set of wicks, the woman placed the rod upon a rack to cool while she repeated the dipping process with another set. Gradually, repeated dippings and coolings built up the layers of wax until a handsome, tapering candle resulted. When one batch was finished, she cut the wicks free from the rod, sliced the bottoms flush with a sharp knife—and there you were.

It didn't take Cousin Alfred long to see the possibilities inherent in this occupation, and it was his proposal that we pool our resources and go into the candle-dipping business. Our resources at the moment consisted of fifty-eight cents, but this was sufficient to enable us to buy a ball of string which was all we felt was needed to begin operations.

That, Cousin Alfred opined, was the beauty of this undertaking. Since the candles sold for twenty cents apiece and one ball of string should make several hundred candles, we could hardly help making a handsome profit on our investment.

With our ball of string from Mr. Atwood's hardware store, we went into business on an August day—a day when Father, Mother and Doris had gone to visit friends in Brewster.

From the candle factory lady, who didn't realize that competition threatened, we had learned that the first step was to pick our bayberries and remove the outer covering of greenish-gray wax by boiling the berries in water. The wax would melt and rise to the top and when cool would harden into a crust which could be removed as pure bayberry wax.

Bayberries were plentiful but, even so, it took quite a while to pick the four ten-quart bucketsful we felt we would need for our first run. Then we set to work on the actual manufacturing process. By this time we even had a corporate name—the Cape Cod Candle Company, Inc.,—and envisioned our profits in the thousands.

Another advantage we enjoyed was the fact that we didn't have to sink additional (and nonexistent) capital into equipment. Mother's lobster kettle served as a receptacle in which to boil the berries, a smaller kettle would hold the melted wax, and a pair of Mother's steel knitting needles served as our wick holders.

The first inkling we had that there might be more to this project than met the eye was when we had boiled the berries on the oil stove and cooled them. From each ten-quart bucket of berries we retrieved a thin film of wax sufficient to make about half a candle. It was Cousin Alfred's suggestion then to add paraffin to the bayberry wax, but we didn't have the price of the paraffin so we had to make do with what we had.

When our entire collection of wax had been melted, Cousin Alfred and I stood over it, each holding a wick tied to a knitting needle. Carefully, we dipped and held the wicks aloft to cool—and discovered the second complication on the road to riches.

The wax adhered to the wick but not in the symmetrical, tapering manner achieved by the candle factory lady. Cousin Alfred's candle grew to look like a lumpy pyramid; mine more nearly resembled a pretzel.

By the time our first two candles were finished, so was the Cape Cod Candle Company, Inc.; but, alas, we found that it was harder to go out of business than to enter it. It took several hours of hard work to clean the kettle that had held the wax and our lobsters tasted of bayberry for the next three weeks.

Father and Mother took a dim view of our enterprise and we were forced to remain at home for a week while our less industrious but perhaps more practical peers—including Doris—walked happily to the village for the evening mail.

Corn Hill in Truro, where the Pilgrims "borrowed" from an Indian cache "as much corne as two men could carry," was good for a brief visit each summer, but of much more interest was another historic site known as First Encounter Beach in Eastham. Here on a low sand cliff overlooking Cape Cod Bay the Pilgrims had had their first meeting with hostile Indians.

This event took place on the morning of December 8, 1620. Two days earlier, eighteen of the *Mayflower*'s company had set out in a shallop from Provincetown, where their ship lay at anchor, to look for a suitable place to settle. Included in the party were twelve Pilgrims, Mate John Clarke, Gunner Robert Coffin and three other sailors of the *Mayflower*'s crew.

Mate Clarke was nominal leader of the group but no one else could be leader when Myles Standish was present, as he was on this occasion. The men were heavily armed, for they were apprehensive concerning the welcome they might receive from the red owners of the land. They had already "borrowed" the corn and perhaps this fact did nothing to allay their anxieties.

On the first day of the trip they had followed the shore of the bay to the present site of Wellfleet where they camped for the night. They spent most of the second day exploring the vicinity so it wasn't until evening that they arrived at Eastham. Here they erected a barricade, brought in firewood, ate their frugal supper and, after posting sentries, went to bed.

Their slumbers were disturbed by disconcerting sounds which one of the sailors, who had been in Newfoundland, assured them were the howling of wolves, but nothing untoward occurred until morning. After their customary prayers, some of the group began preparing breakfast while others carried baggage down to the shallop. Some even took their muskets, although Myles Standish cautioned against this recklessness.

Dawn was whitening the east and the little band had just sat down to breakfast when, all of a sudden, they heard the same blood-chilling cries that had alarmed them in the night.

A chronicler of the event has described the cries as "Woach! Ha! Ha! Woach!"—sounds which wolves seldom, if ever, utter. If the startled campers still thought the cries were made by wolves they were quickly disabused by the sudden appearance of the sentries running for their lives, pursued by a shower of flint-tipped arrows.

"Indians!" they shouted, dashing into the barricade.

Myles Standish and several others who had kept their muskets with them fired in the direction of the hidden sounds. Others of the beleaguered group ran toward the shallop to recover their weapons, whereupon a band of

Indians burst from the woods to cut them off. A group of Pilgrims ran to their companions' aid, armed with cutlasses, and drove the Indians off. But one "lustie" redskin "and no less valiante" stood his ground and loosed several arrows into the stockade.

This was too much for the short-fused Captain Standish who took a careful bead and sent bark and twigs showering about the enemy's ears. With that, the savage "gave an extraordinary shrike and away went they all of them." The Pilgrims pursued them a short distance, shouting and firing their guns to show them that "they were not afrade of them."

Today a granite boulder with a bronze tablet marks the site of this brief skirmish. The sheltering woods are gone now, but when we first visited the spot it must otherwise have looked much as it did on the morning when the attack occurred. Today a town bathing beach and a number of cottages on the bluff detract somewhat from the pristine sense of history.

Almost three hundred years later, another enemy attack —this one at Nauset—resulted in another historic Cape Cod site. It was Sunday morning, July 21, 1918, and most of the good people of Orleans were in church. Off Nauset Inlet a tugboat puffed its way southward along the coast with three empty coal barges in tow.

Suddenly, the waters parted and a German U-boat surfaced several hundred yards from the barges. There were no other vessels in sight so the submarine's commander turned his attention and his guns upon the luckless tow. From 10:30 until noon the U-boat lay upon the surface and fired 147 shells, eventually sinking the three barges but not the tug.

At first, the few people on the beach thought one of our submarines was engaging in target practice upon barges provided for the purpose. The surprised barge crews knew better, however, and they promptly took to boats and rowed ashore.

Someone on the beach, being apprised of the true situation, called the Naval Aviation Training Camp at Chatham, only to be told that its personnel had gone to a baseball game in Provincetown. The base did muster one seaplane which in due course arrived over the scene. Unfortunately, the pilot had no bombs nor machine guns so he contented himself with dropping a large monkey wrench which, had it hit the captain, would have done him no good. Instead, it fell harmlessly into the sea and the German skipper made an obscene gesture at the plane.

All along the Atlantic coast ships remained in port until it became apparent that this was just an isolated occurrence and a warning from the Imperial German Government.

We missed this episode and only arrived after it had ended, to stand looking out over the sea at the recent battlefield, the only scene of hostilities on this side of the ocean in World War I. Today a tablet marks the site at a spot where one of the U-boat shells struck the shoreline dunes. The rippled circle marking the spot where the monkey wrench missed the U-boat captain is gone.

Clam Chowder
to Crème Brûlée

AT INTERVALS during the summer Cap'n Davis's chickens, our clams, perch, pickerel, tautog and even Cap'n Lombard's lobsters began to pall and when this occurred we used to look forward to dining out. Curiously, whenever we did so, we always seemed to end up ordering clams or lobster; but, as Mother said, different cooking made things taste different and, once in a while, it was good to eat away from home. The problem was in finding a place to go.

Cape Cod today offers the visitor a plenitude of eating places of all varieties from clam bars and hamburger stands to deluxe restaurants featuring *haute cuisine*. It was not always so. In the earlier years of the century establishments offering food and drink to the traveler were few and far between, once you crossed the Cape Cod Canal.

Some of the summer hotels, like the Chequesset Inn, served meals to transient guests, and there were perhaps a dozen restaurants open for business, but Sam's Drive-In, Pete's Place, the Lobster Potte, Chick'n-N-The-Ruff, Ye Olde Snacke Shacke and similar oases lay in the still distant future.

The scarcity of restaurants, however, was compensated for by the high standards of those which existed. The cuisine in most of them was not exactly *haute* but it was ample, well-prepared and hearty. When you pushed yourself away from their tables you knew that you had dined.

Such a place was Camp Opeechee on the shores of Lake Wequaquet at Centerville, a gastronomic stronghold which we came upon quite by accident. It was the summer of 1915 and the Pope-Hartford had been especially temperamental on the journey to the Cape.

On the first day of the trip, owing to a puncture, a blowout and a carburetor malfunction, dusk overtook us at North Attleboro. The second day was half spent by the time repairs had been effected and late afternoon found us still on the wrong side of the Canal.

To make matters worse, it was raining. Cousin Alfred and I were not speaking to one another, Doris was not speaking to anyone, Father was gripping the wheel in tense determination and Mother was nursing a headache. It was still Father's conviction that we could make Wellfleet that night, but Mother had other ideas. Finally, as we rolled through Sandwich, she gave expression to them.

"George," she said, and when she called Father George instead of Doc, it meant that she had had it. "I think we should stop somewhere for the night. The children are cranky, I'm worn out and there's no sense in killing ourselves to get to the cottage tonight. It will be there tomorrow."

She used the proper approach. Had she suggested that Father might be too tired to continue, he would have driven all night, but when she put it on this basis. . . .

"Very well," he replied, a little stiffly. "Where do you suggest that we stop?"

This was a very good question, for hostelries were practically non-existent in the area and motels and over-night cabins had not yet been invented.

"We could drive to Falmouth," Mother said.

"What's the sense in going twenty miles out of our way?" Father demanded. "We might as well. . . ."

And just then we saw a sign that said, "Wequaquet Inn, Centerville 5 M."

"There!" Mother exclaimed, and her exclamation summed up the situation, once and for all.

We drove to Centerville and after a few inquiries arrived at the Wequaquet Inn. The young woman who greeted us was sympathetic but dubious.

"Oh, dear," she murmured, "I'm sorry, but we're full up. The storm, you know." She hesitated, frowning. "I hate to turn you away on a night like this. . . ." She pondered and then brightened: "Maybe they'd take you over at the lake."

"The lake?" Father prompted.

The woman nodded. "Camp Opeechee. It's an eating place we run on Lake Wequaquet. Let me call them and see."

Soon she came back smiling. "They said to come along," she reported, "if you'll put up with what they've got. We don't usually put folks up at the camp, but there's a couple of spare rooms."

She gave us directions to the lake and we set out again. By now darkness had fallen and the wind and rain had increased.

"First road to the right," the woman had told us.

This turned out to be a cartpath entered through a pasture gate and we were sure this couldn't have been the thoroughfare she had in mind. It was, however, as we learned by trial and error, and so we began lurching and splashing along its rutted surface through thick pine woods.

Just when it seemed certain that we must have lost our

way and would shortly find ourselves at a dead end with no way to turn around, we came into a clearing in the middle of which stood a shadowy building with lamps burning in the windows.

Gratefully we piled out and climbed the front steps to a wide verandah. The door opened in answer to our knock and a plump, middle-aged woman ushered us into the foyer.

"We were expecting you," she said. "Terrible night, isn't it? I'll show you your rooms and then, when you're ready, you can have some supper. I'm afraid you'll have to take what we have," she added apologetically.

"That's all right," Mother assured her. "Anything you have will be fine."

Her words were prophetic, for a half-hour later when we were seated at a table in the spacious dining room overlooking the lake, the middle-aged woman opened the proceedings by bringing each of us a bowl of clam chowder with crackers and hot biscuits.

We thought that was to be our supper and were duly grateful but then the woman reappeared with plates of steamed clams, complete with broth and drawn butter. We had just finished the clams and broth when she returned once more, this time with five broiled live lobsters. To these she added French fried potatoes, string beans and a tossed salad.

By now Cousin Alfred and I were conversing freely and Doris was able to smile enigmatically. Mother was feeling better and Father opined generously that he was glad Mother had suggested stopping overnight.

"I was beginning to feel a little tired myself," he admitted, attacking a lobster claw.

By the time the meal had ended with blueberry pie à la

mode and coffee, a spirit of camaraderie prevailed, and the rigors of the journey and the storm had been forgotten. The bill for the meal, incidentally, was a dollar apiece.

This was our introduction to Camp Opeechee and for the next ten years or so until the place closed, we made a point of going there two or three times a summer for dinner. By the end of this time, owing to the rising cost of living, the price of the meal had gone up to a dollar and a half, but it was still worth every cent of the charge.

The restaurant grew through the years and attracted more and more people to its scenic location until the owner's wife died in a tragic accident and this landmark came to an end.

Among the *plus haute* cuisine on Cape Cod at the time, perhaps, was the Eagleston Inn at Hyannis. Its dinners progressed along lines similar to those of Camp Opeechee, but the surroundings were much more posh and the decor considerably more impressive.

Situated almost in the center of town, the attractive shingled inn was furnished with rare antiques and reflected in its interior decorations the taste and flair of the proprietor, Mrs. Eagleston, who also owned a smart shop across the street.

Our occasional trips to Hyannis and the Eagleston Inn were red-letter days on our summer calendar, but they demanded a price. The price, for Cousin Alfred and me, was to invest ourselves in white duck knickerbockers, blue serge jackets and white shirts complete with Buster Brown collars—high, stiffly starched yokes patterned, I am sure, after torture instruments of the Inquisition and popularized by a repulsive character then in vogue in the nation's comic strips.

In that simpler day, public places of the better sort, including restaurants, assumed that their patrons would do them the courtesy of dressing in a suitable manner, an assumption to which the patrons also subscribed. There was no need for a public house to have a row of jackets handy for those who appeared in shirtsleeves for no one would have dreamed of showing up in shirtsleeves or tieless, any more than they would have appeared trouserless.

In preparation for our trips to Hyannis, Father donned white flannels and blue serge jacket, or a Palm Beach suit, and put on his Panama hat. Mother wore a striped voile dress and ostrich-trimmed hat or sometimes a white faille. My sister Doris loved these excursions to Hyannis for they enabled her to put on her Gretchen model muslin dress and the wide, beribboned straw hat Mother had bought her in Boston, and also because there was always the possibility, if she played her cards right, that she might be allowed to purchase additional finery in the Hyannis shops.

Another price Cousin Alfred and I had to pay was that of the obligatory bath that preceded the duck knickerbockers, serge jackets and Buster Brown collars. In the ordinary course of events, we were allowed to take a cake of soap and clean underwear on our fishing trips to the ponds and take our baths in their pure soft waters.

But for trips to Hyannis hot tub baths were requisite. And a hot tub bath at our cottage was a production. First we had to get the tin tub from the closet off the kitchen and pump sufficient water to fill it partway. It took several bucketfuls to achieve the desired quantity. To this was added a kettleful of boiling water from the kitchen stove. If the resulting mixture was too hot, you had to pump more water. If it was too cool, more water had to be heated while you shivered wet and naked in the middle of the kitchen. And when you had finished, you had to empty out the bath water and clean the tub.

Cousin Alfred sometimes tried to short-circuit these time-consuming steps by washing only those portions of his anatomy which would be exposed when he had dressed, but this deception was easily unmasked by having him roll up his sleeves or take off his stockings, and he was summarily ordered back to the kitchen to complete his ablutions.

But, at last, all was in readiness, and the Pope-Hartford sat panting in the yard. Bathed, coifed, groomed and costumed, we would take our places and with a clash of gears we were off. Sometimes the Andover boy went with us and upon these occasions Cousin Alfred's and my spirits fell in a direct ratio to the rise of Doris's.

For the Andover boy made us feel our callow immaturity and our inferiority. He was all of seventeen and worldly. His conversation was wont to stray from frogs, turtles and

fish to Beethoven, Michelangelo and someone known as Swinburne. He thought the Cape quaint and its residents *simpatico.*

He also had the irritating habit of suffixing his observations with "Don't you think so, Mrs. Janes?" or "Do you feel the same way, Doctor?" He seldom addressed Cousin Alfred and me except to inquire patronizingly as to our juvenile activities. In his company, however, Doris became trustworthy, loyal, helpful, friendly, courteous, obedient and cheerful—traits she had promised the Girl Scouts to embrace but which she did not always exhibit in the bosom of the family.

Hyannis was in some ways an even more fascinating place than Provincetown. It was, and is, the metropolis of Cape Cod and, even in those days, its main street was crowded with traffic. Sometimes you had to drive a block or two to find a place to park and, as you crept along, you would pass by cars from practically every state in the whole forty-eight–state Union. There they reposed in their splendor beside the curb—Appersons, Chalmers, Paiges, Locomobiles, Pierce Arrows, Packards, Cadillacs, Stanley Steamers, Stevens Duryeas, Buicks, Fords, yes, and Pope-Hartfords, many driven by liveried chauffeurs.

The Hyannis stores were different from those of Provincetown, too. There were a few souvenir shops but the majority bore such names as Abercrombie & Fitch, Mark Cross, Filene's and Stowell.

Upon our arrival in Hyannis, our procedure was to leave Mother and Doris in front of one of the shops while Father, Cousin Alfred and I continued on to Hyannisport to view the estates sprawled along the shore. Some of them were hidden away behind high walls so that you could only catch fleeting glimpses of wooded grounds through the gates. Others, though, with their formal gardens, spreading shade trees and winding drives framing huge brick or wooden homes, were open to view.

Best of all was the drive along the harbor behind whose rocky breakwater at least two or three private steam yachts always rode at anchor. No cabin cruisers these but, rather, true ocean-going vessels as large, at least, as the *Dorothy Bradford* and manned by crews of two dozen or more men.

This inspection of homes and yachts consumed an hour or two and then it was time to rejoin Mother and my sister Doris. Usually this rendezvous took a little while to effect because, engrossed in their shopping, the ladies would lose all track of time and fail to arrive at the designated meeting place at the appointed hour. Then Cousin Alfred would set out in one direction while I took another and sooner or later one or the other of us would flush our quarry from some millinery counter or rack of shirtwaists.

Now it was time for all of us to take a leisurely tour through Abercrombie & Fitch's emporium. Mother and my sister Doris saved this till we had rejoined them, for this was one shop that Father and Cousin Alfred and I enjoyed visiting, too. We could and did spend many absorbing hours inspecting the beach equipment, athletic gear, picnic utensils and games on display at Abercrombie's.

And, finally, with appetites whetted by these activities, we would wander over to the Eagleston Inn for dinner.

Although the food at the Eagleston Inn was in many ways similar to the fare we enjoyed at Camp Opeechee, it was served on translucent bone china plates and the glassware was choice crystal. Cousin Alfred and I were admonished to let discretion overcome enthusiasm in our handling of these costly appointments.

"Sit up to the table and pay attention," I believe was the way Mother worded her request.

A finger bowl with warm water and a wedge of lemon accompanied the steamed clams, a grape leaf underlay the cut glass bowl which held the drawn butter, and a dab of whipped cream floated upon the surface of the clam broth.

The main course consisted of lobsters—broiled, Thermidor or salad—and the only concession made to those soulless beings who didn't care for these unsurpassed crustaceans was the substitution for them of broiled chicken.

In the matter of lobster, though, garnished with parsley and sprinkled with lightly browned crumbs or stuffed with a delectable cheese sauce or again fashioned into a triumphant salad, the Eagleston Inn knew no peers.

The chef selected two-pound lobsters and one time when a heavy run on these delicacies had exhausted the supply so that only five two-pound lobsters remained for our party of six, he sent our waitress in with two pound-and-a-half lobsters on the sixth plate. The Andover boy was with us and, while Cousin Alfred and I gazed hungrily at this unexpected bonanza, Mother took charge.

"I'm sure this young man could eat two lobsters," she said, indicating not Cousin Alfred and not me but the Andover boy, who heartily concurred.

The Eagleston Inn desserts were masterpieces worthy of climaxing all that had gone before—not apple pie à la mode or blancmange, but baked Alaskas, *crèmes brûlées*, Charlotte Russes and incomparable parfaits. Necessarily, such fare came high and even in the early days, the price of dinner at the Eagleston Inn was two dollars per person.

Considerably less *haute* but just as excellent in its own way was an establishment in South Wellfleet which called itself the Adams House, perhaps in light-hearted imitation of the famous Boston hostelry of that name or, possibly, because the proprietor's name was Adams.

The South Wellfleet Adams House was somewhat different. It was housed in a simple, white shedlike frame building and consisted of a dining room and a kitchen—no lounge, no porch, no frills of any sort. The walls were unfinished, the rafters showed overhead, and one sat at round wooden tables covered with red-and-white checked cloths. Crockery and glassware were thick and durable, the cutlery utilitarian—but the food was out of this world.

Lobsters of a lurid crimson hue, together with attempted likenesses of fish, clams and oysters, painted by a local artist on the exterior walls gave promise of the viands to be found within.

The menu was long and part of the pleasure of reading it was in discovering the several ways the management had found to take liberties with traditional spelling. Quahaugs sometimes came out *cwohogs* and steamed clams as *steemed* but you knew what the compiler had in mind. And the spelling detracted no whit from the finished product.

The proprietor, a short, ebullient man with a wisp of gray hair and a disarming manner, was born thirty years too soon. In a later day he would have been a topflight maitre d' and, even as it was, he did all right. Doubling as head chef, he still found time to greet customers and also to appear frequently during one's meal to comment on the food and to explain its preparation. One practically dined with Mr. Adams looking over one's shoulder.

His comments were forthright and to the point. The freshness of his raw materials and the wholesomeness of his ingredients were fetishes of Mr. Adams.

It is still the fashion today, despite some heartening trends to the contrary, to debunk the "good old days" and to detail at some length all the things that were wrong with them. In the matter of food, for example, housewives are advised to consider how many hours their grandmothers spent over a hot wood range to turn out dishes less delectable than their present-day frozen or canned counterparts. This is, of course, hogwash.

To generations brought up on ersatz products—"Essence of clam, magnesium chloride, calcium chloride, ferrous sulfate, potassium chloride, potato, imitation onion flavor, artificially colored"—these modern concoctions, whose contents read more like the inventory of a drugstore prescription counter than the ingredients of a dish for human consumption, have become normal and accustomed fare. But I wish they had known Mr. Adams.

Mr. Adams used to say, "If a clam don't flinch when I knife it, it don't go in my chowder."

And he would stand over us, watching as we took our first spoonfuls and then ask, "How does that taste, Doc?" And when Father replied that it was delicious Mr. Adams would nod. "It ought to be, b'god. It's got a quart of cream and a pound of butter in it besides a quart of quahaugs." Essence of clam, forsooth!

At the Adams House you could order cwohogs on the half-shell (Mr. Adams didn't call them Littlenecks), cwohog chowder, steemed clams, clam fritters, clam cakes and fried clams, and besides his dealings in clams, Mr. Adams trafficked heavily in fish—mackerel, swordfish, haddock, flounder, porgies, butterfish, halibut, pollock, cod and bluefish. Each individual fish had to pass his rigid inspection. Bluefish were especially suspect.

"They got to be fresh," he insisted, "or else they ain't worth cooking. You take them Boston restaurants. Boat catches the bluefish on Monday morning, say, and don't land 'em till afternoon. They lay on ice overnight. Restaurant buys 'em next morning and don't serve 'em till that night. By then they ain't fit to eat. The bluefish on my menu this afternoon was swimming this morning."

Mr. Adams offered several choices of shore dinners. His Number One Shore Dinner—at $1.75 a plate—provided seven courses. You started with clams on the half shell and proceeded to a cup of quahaug chowder. Next came steamed clams and then fried clams, followed by a fish course. Then you had a choice of broiled live or boiled lobster, lobster in butter or lobster salad, along with French fried potatoes, after which those who could went on to pie and/or ice cream. If you bogged down somewhere along the line, the rest of your dinner went home with you in a sack—Mr. Adams didn't call it a doggie bag.

By no means the least rewarding of our dining out experiences on Cape Cod was our occasional attendance at the local church suppers. Two or three times a month placards would appear in the windows of Mr. Wiley's store, Nye's Souvenir Shop and Cap'n Lombard's fish market—"Supper. Friday, July 29 at 6:00 P.M. Admission 30 cents."

Sometimes the placards emanated from the Congregational Church, sometimes the Methodist. In either case, the culinary standards were equal. The high price of 30 cents, which caused comment in vestry circles, was a reflection of the fact that July and August were the best months in which to fill the coffers of the Ladies Guild and the Sisterhood, since everyone knew that summer folks didn't care how much they paid for a good meal.

The meals were good, no doubt of that. While their inland sisters put on baked bean suppers, these Cape Cod women, raised beside the sea, turned their considerable talents to clam chowder and quahaug pies. The Congregationalists specialized in the former, the Methodists pinned their star to the latter.

On the afternoon of the chowder suppers, the ladies gathered in the church kitchen, donned their aprons and went to work peeling potatoes and onions, dicing salt pork and mincing quahaugs opened on the spot by some male parishioner coerced into helping out. Some of these ladies were the same ones who concocted flavorsome chowders for the Cape Cod Clam Chowder Club outings on Billingsgate Island. All were equally expert. Any one of them would have considered essence of clam an abomination before the Lord and its use in one of her chowders a mortal, if not a carnal, sin which would have cost her her chance of Heaven.

By quarter of six all was in readiness and when you entered the parish house where the long, paper-covered tables had been set up, you were greeted with a delicious aroma of steaming chowder. Troops of small fry ran screaming around the tables in games of tag while the adults gathered in little knots to discuss the weather and topics of the day.

"Gettin' so's you can't afford sugar any longer at twenty-five cents a pound. I declare I don't know where it's all going to end."

"Well, I hear they're getting fifty cents a bushel for quahaugs right at the dock."

Promptly at six, a general surging movement toward the tables began and everyone stood behind his chair awaiting the minister's invocation.

The Congregational minister liked to use these opportunities to impress summer visitors with his oratorical abilities and sometimes his blessing lengthened into something more nearly approaching a sermon—or so it seemed to me, hungrily sniffing the kitchen aromas. But at length he finished conveying our gratitude and his *Amen* was drowned by the scraping of chairs, the buzz of resumed conversation and the entrance of a procession of ladies bearing trays loaded with bowls of fragrant chowder.

While you consumed the chowder, along with pilot crackers, several ladies went about pouring coffee while others patrolled the room, alert for an empty bowl to be refilled—as Mrs. Eaton said, "If we're going to charge 'em thirty cents, the least we can do is see they get enough to eat."

If one didn't, it was his own fault, for the chowder course was followed by a dessert of homemade pies. There were apple pies, cherry pies, lemon, chocolate, mince, apricot, prune, gooseberry, blueberry, cocoanut cream, banana cream and custard pies, and in their fabrication and baking each cook tried to outdo all the other suppliers so that the result turned into a pie-making contest. Consequently, each lady was hurt if one didn't sample her contribution. It all added up to quite a lot of pie consumption before the meal ended.

Afterwards, for those able to remain awake, there was usually some sort of entertainment, either living tableaux by the members of the Junior Sunday School, musical numbers by the church quartet, or readings of poetry selections by the minister. One way or another, you certainly received your thirty cents worth from one of these suppers.

The proceedings at the Methodist Church suppers were similar, except that there you were served quahaug pie and johnnycake instead of chowder and pilot crackers. And for dessert, perhaps because you had already had pie or perhaps because they didn't wish to copy the Congregationalists, the Methodist ladies featured cakes—chocolate cake, devil's food cake, angel cake, spice cake, fig cake, cream cake, sponge cake, raised cake, pound cake, orange cake, and lemon cake among them.

And again you were urged to eat as much cake as you wished and when you had done so, if there were any cakes left, the thrifty Methodists auctioned them off during the evening. On more than one occasion Cousin Alfred and I pooled our resources and bid in a cake which we ate later in the privacy of our bedroom.

And, finally, while we didn't "dine out" at the Curran House at Wellfleet, we "breakfasted out" there once a year. The Curran House on Holbrook Avenue was a low, rambling structure run by an ex–sea captain, Cap'n James Curran, and each Labor Day morning we used to breakfast there before leaving for home. This was so that we didn't have to take time to do dishes before starting our journey.

Cap'n Curran began serving breakfast at six o'clock and

we were on hand when the dining room doors opened. Breakfast, let it be said, was not an orange-juice-and-black-coffee affair at the Curran House. Under Cap'n Curran's forthright auspices breakfast began with hot cereal and proceeded from there to griddle cakes and sausages or bacon. Then, and only then, were you ready for your baked potatoes and scrod or creamed codfish. Blueberry or corn muffins accompanied this course and hot doughnuts completed the meal.

Not a bad breakfast for thirty-five cents and a breakfast which materially helped to mitigate our depression at leaving Cape Cod for another long year.

"I See
by the Bee"

THE NOON train brought the Boston papers to the Cape and these gave us news of the happenings in the world outside—the sweep of German armies through Belgium, the first ship through the Panama Canal, the Black Tom explosion in New Jersey and the death of President Warren G. Harding. But for more intimate news of events that went on all around us, we depended upon the weekly appearance of the *Cape Cod Item & Bee*.

The *Bee* came out on Thursdays in Hyannis and in its pages you could learn all that had happened between Sandwich and Provincetown during the preceding week, as well as some of the things that were expected to happen during the coming week. Each village had its reporter and no event, however small, escaped Your Correspondent's eagle eye.

Our copies of the *Bee* were delivered in the early days by Cap'n Higgins, who, though he had never quite attained to this rank during his seafaring days, had been a gunner's mate in the United States Navy during the Civil War and was among those present with Admiral Farragut at the Battle of Mobile Bay.

He claimed a close acquaintance with "Old Salamander," as he called the Admiral, and he liked to recall his commander's famous words, which he rendered as, "Damn them torpeters! Full steam ahead!"

Now a wizened but spry seventy-four, Cap'n Higgins was something of an entrepreneur. Not only did he deliver the *Bee* but he also carried on his delivery route a market basket of vegetables and fruits in season.

Before he gave up your paper he would always inquire, "Like to buy some nice rhubub today?" or "How about a nice summer sqush?" and, somehow, it seemed ungenerous not to buy his wares, aside from the fact that you felt you might not get your paper if you didn't.

When you had made your purchase, Cap'n Higgins was ready to discuss the news of the day. "I see by the *Bee*," was the way he invariably introduced the subject, and then he would go on to regale us so thoroughly with the local intelligence that, as Father said, by the time he had sold you the paper you didn't really need to read it.

But this wasn't quite so, for he contented himself with relating the more important items, such as Theodore Roosevelt's visit to Provincetown, leaving the social columns for your later perusal.

There was quite a lot to peruse. Here, unvarnished and [sic], we find that:

Miss Laura Newcomb has a new piano. It is upright.

Little Fannie Paine of Beach Plum Lane is entertaining la grippe. Not a very pleasant guest, eh, Fannie?

For mild, easy action of the bowels, try Doane's Laxative, 30 cents at all stores.

Mr. and Mrs. Kenneth Warren of Brookline opened

their cottage at Nauset Heights on Saturday. This was the first time they have been lit this season.

Willis C. Crowell of Jamaica Plain came down last Friday but returned home on the afternoon train.

Mr. and Mrs. Asa Higgins of this place went to call on Mr. and Mrs. Ned Eaton on Tuesday evening at their home on Mayo Road, but when they got there no one was at home.

Can it be that casting bread upon the waters is what makes the dark, blue ocean roll?

Friday's sultriness was followed by a delightfully cool evening. The weather right now is delicious.

Mrs. Loren Strong of Chequesset Neck fell down her back steps and bruised her landing. Dr. Bell says she is just lucky there were no more steps.

The weather here is delightful and many of the visitors who are here at present remarked on the atmosphere and its invigorating effect, but this ozonic quality is not confined to Yarmouthport. It is a peculiarity of the Cape.

A hungry and seedy tramp was found on the beach yesterday and taken to one of the life-saving stations by the patrol. His appearance indicated a long fast and he was invited to eat. The following helped in a measure to appease his appetite: a large piece of ham with six eggs, four slices of boiled beef and four potatoes, one mince pie, one apple pie, a quarter-pound of cheese, eighteen doughnuts and eight cups of coffee with bread and butter ad libitum.

Two pups—young seals—have been shot in the harbor the past few weeks. They have been presented to the town clerk who gets three dollars per head or tail for them.

Edwin Rich, having looked upon the wine when it was red or some other color, and become pugnacious, was fined $2 and put under bond of $200 by Judge Reynolds which, not being able to procure, he is spending a short season for reflection at Jailer Leterney's hotel.

Mr. Chandler Morris is in town and is a gust at Mrs. Alice Newcomb's.

Miss Lina Thompson of Pamet Point is looking for pupils in pianoforte. Miss Thompson can play other things, too.

Closing exercises of the Yarmouth High School were held at the school Wednesday afternoon. Principal Pierce presided. The march by the piano and cornet, played by Principal Pierce and Clifton Jones, introduced the pupils who, after taking their seats, sang to Principal Pierce's accompaniment "The Warrior Bold."

Chester M. Baker chose "America's Four Hundred Years" as the subject of his paper. This composition possessed a decidedly literary flavor, containing some striking passages showing marked skill in construction and was as patriotic in tone as the most intense American could wish. Many of the smooth-running sentences and well-rounded periods exhibited a facility with the pen that would have done credit to maturer years and riper experience.

His essay was followed by the song "Strangers Yet" by the school, accompanied by Principal Pierce. Diplomas were handed to the graduating class by Principal Pierce who then with Clifton Jones played the stirring strains of "Pomp and Circumstance" while the pupils marched out.

The glorious Fourth was celebrated by the most perfect weather, though a storm of wind and rain threatened. The parade started at the town pump, making a circuit of the town and stopping at the home of James Swett at the north end where it was regaled with lemonade. Returning, a speech was made at the post office by Mr. C. A. Collins who wore a veritable hat of the year of the War of 1812 for the occasion, after which the crowd dispersed to breakfast of which they must have stood in great need.

The Old Colony District Grange met with the East Sandwich Grange July 25. It was not as interesting as usual, but with music by the Grange and recitations by Will Elwell and Mrs. Howland, a vocal solo by Miss Terrill and a discussion "Shall agriculture be taught in our public schools?" the afternoon was pleasantly passed.

Joseph Chase has a heifer which gives twelve quarts of milk a day. First calf.

The Sisterhood of the Methodist Church will serve a Quahaug Pie Supper in the church parlor on Wednesday evening, August 5, at six o'clock. Mrs. William Snow will be in charge of pies and Mrs. Benjamin Pearse of cakes.

Those contributing pies who wish to do so may bake themselves at home, but are requested not to put potatoes in them as was done by some at the last supper. Pies should be delivered to the church kitchen hot by five-thirty. Cakes will be received after three-thirty. Admission will be 35 cents for adults, twenty-five cents for children under 12.

Mrs. Robert Baker was the recipient of two chickens for the Fourth. The bread she cast upon the water is returning to her again.

Tuesday evening was observed as Flora's month at the Grange. Mrs. Maria Armstrong holding that office presided in a very charming manner. Each member had been requested to bring a bouquet of flowers in competition for a prize and each lady two buttonhole bouquets just alike, one of which was deposited in Flora's basket and the other which she was to wear.

The gentlemen chosen as a committee to decide on the prettiest arrangement were J. S. Carlson, E. F. Stiff, W. C. Fish, J. T. Howland. First prize, a watering pot, went to Mrs. Lemuel Jones, second prize, a trowel, to Mrs. Armstrong.

Refreshments consisting of lemonade, bananas and vanilla creams were then served. The entertainment was very interesting, consisting of recitations and music and each lady gave the origin and manner of culture of some flowers from her bouquet.

Mrs. H. P. Lovell of North Road contributes unwittingly to the entertainment of the Hallet House guests when her melodious voice is wafted on the summer breezes from her retreat on the hill. Thus far the wary bluefish is conspicuous by his absence.

Miss Leslie Cahoon is at home.

Mrs. T. P. Henderson is about the same.

Fire Chief Mortimer Sears has asked that those who took boots from the fire station to wear scalloping return them at once. If a fire broke out they would be needed and remember, it could be your house. Fair play, fellows!

Capt. James T. Baker has joined the schooner *Clarence Fenner* for the season and has sailed, tight, for Philadelphia.

Richard Fish of Boston was held in $1,000 bond in the Municipal Criminal Court Saturday morning for appearance next Friday on a charge of embezzlement. Fish has had a checkered career. Having resided at West Barnstable, he removed to Provincetown. It is said that in Provincetown his principal occupation was poker playing in which he was very successful, the youth of the town having been his "willing (?)" victims.

Hearing that a warrant was out for his arrest, he put in an appearance and was informed that he should go to headquarters and give himself up. The question is whether Fish's proverbial good luck will stand by him and he again escape the punishment which, if the above is true, he richly deserves or not.

Mr. Ben Rich ran his boat *Gull* into a rock in Wellfleet Bay and sank it.

Henry Fuller and wife narrowly escaped a serious accident Friday. Mrs. Fuller was seated in their carriage. As Mr. Fuller got in the horse started suddenly, throwing Mr. Fuller to the ground. He was taken up insensible. The horse was fortunately stopped long enough to get Mrs. Fuller out when he started for home, smashing the carriage into fragments. It was lucky no serious damage was done.

Personal: I want a husband not less than 50 years old. I am 40 years old, weight 150 pounds, height 5′5″, Protestant seamstress, dark complexion, have no property. Have good health, never been married, play the piano slightly, fair singer.

Mrs. Ephrain Crowell had two severe haemmorhages from the head on Friday week, a second attack being so profuse as to appear alarming and to require the aid of a physician. She is about her work as usual and seems to realize no ill effect from it. On the contrary, it may prove beneficial.

Mr. Alexander B. Chase's horse died very suddenly last Sunday evening. He had been in good health up to then.

Ken Howes was thrown from the wagon of Gus Warham a few days ago and came within one of breaking his neck.

A burglar made a visit to the building of the First

National Bank in this town a little after midnight Sunday. Bank President Davis's hired girl, Nellie McSweeney, occupies a chamber over the bank.

About half-past twelve she was awakened by a noise and realized at once that someone was in her room. Half frozen with terror, she exclaimed, "Holy Mother! Who's there?"

"Hush!" commanded a hoarse voice. "I've been chased in here."

The girl, recovering her presence of mind, began to scream and knock on the wall, although she had little hope of being heard by members of the Davis family who occupy a portion of the building somewhat remote from where her room is located.

The burglar attempted to prevent her from screaming by placing his hand over her mouth and threatening her but she did not desist in her outcry. Pretending she heard someone coming, she exclaimed, "Oh, Mr. Davis! I'm so glad you're coming!"

On hearing these words, the fellow released her and made for the window by which he had evidently entered. Just then there came a flash of summer lightning which plainly revealed his person. A moment later he was gone. The girl says his clothing was ragged and he emitted a strong odor of tobacco and fish. He broke the window in getting out and disarranged some plants and pots beneath the window either in getting in or out.

Mr. Davis thinks he expected to get into the bank and, ignorant of the precautions which are always taken in institutions of this kind, hoped to find some loose money lying around.

About an hour later a burglar, perhaps the same one,

made an attempt to enter the house of Edward Warner. Miss Nellie Warner was awakened by feeling a breath of cold air upon her face. She was startled and alarmed as she knew she had closed the window before going to bed. Looking to her window, she saw it being cautiously raised. Thoroughly frightened, she screamed for her father on which the window was dropped and the burglar decamped.

If this fellow keeps prowling about Yarmouthport, he will stumble into the wrong room some night and put the medical examiner of the district to the trouble of holding an autopsy over his miserable carcass.

The Bible says that cleanliness is next to godliness. Such being the case, we're afraid there is room for some missionary work right here at our own doorstep. If the dirty and greasy condition of many of the library books are to be taken into account, a little more care and neatness in the handling of books is apparently needed. Several volumes, besides being extremely dirty, have also been generously supplied with the broken fragments of lunches.

The first baseball game of the season was played at Plymouth on Saturday. Our boys were victorious, the score at the end of seven innings being 23 to 0.

Charles E. Rich deserted his wife in Brewster and killed himself for love of a girl in Boston.

The feature of the recent Grange meeting was the singing of Mrs. Ada May Benzing, famous contralto of Boston. Mrs. Benzing has a rich, deep contralto voice which penetrated to every corner of the hall. Her enunciation was very clear and distinct, denoting the true artist which she is. In "Behold, I Stand at the Door" by Giude, Mrs. Benzing struck low D. Although she had contracted a severe cold, every note was rendered clear and distinct. She responded to an encore with "Dreams" which was also artistically rendered.

Mr. Benzing's success was as complete. He also came in for a measure of the applause. His rendition of "Awake!" by Nevins was magnificent. In response to an encore he gave the "Lost Chord" by Sullivan. Of course, Mr. and Mrs. Benzing delighted in receiving such warmth of applause but then, they deserve it.

While Elijah Cobb was out berrying last week he came in contact with a large snake. Before he was fully aware of it, the reptile was crawling up the inside of his trouser leg. Mr. Cobb says, "I grasped his head firmly from the outside and endeavored to break his hold but the harder I tugged, the tighter the fellow twisted his coils about my limb."

After struggling for some time, Mr. Cobb broke his hold and ran for the road in an exhausted and fainting condition. He remembers seeing the reptile crawl swiftly away in the opposite direction.

At the time he did not have mind or strength enough to pursue and kill him as he was badly bitten at the groin and his leg was black and blue where the snake had twisted about it. The snake was at least six feet long and four inches through. This reminds your correspondent of one of about the same dimensions which she killed on Great Hill several years ago.

Just prior to the regular celebration of the Holy Communion at the Methodist Church last Sunday the members engaged in an old-fashioned love feast which was most profitable to all present.

Fresh shad is offered for sale in town today. The shad is a highly esteemed dainty at this season. It is in the shad that we find the first roes of summer!

Two young ladies are wanted at the Item office to learn to set type. If one of them has had experience it will do no harm. Apply at once.

Capt. Ralph Cobb has bought the old Mayo place. He is now making extensive repairs in his interior.

"What's the matter? Where are the people running to? Dunno. Guess it must be a fire or a school of mackerel has struck in." A number of people were seen running at the top of their speed down to the marsh opposite the Congregational Church Sunday afternoon and this was the cause of the inquiries and reply given above.

It turned out to be neither one nor the other, but the unfortunate predicament of a horse belonging to Joseph Walker. He stumbled into a mudhole near the baseball grounds and sunk up to his ears, waving vigorously these appendages as signals of distress.

How to get him out? There were as many opinions as there were people present. One man ran for ropes, another divested himself of his clothing and plunged boldly in to the horse's rescue. Seeing that help was coming, the horse apparently decided to take matters into his own hooves. Humping himself and waving his ears, he walked cooly and muddily out of his predicament, leaving his would-be benefactor fast in the hole. Using the ropes originally intended for rescuing the horse, the mired townsman was hauled to safety and the crowd slowly dispersed.

Henry Holbrook of Holbrook Avenue became the innocent victim of an unfortunate accident on Saturday when he went duck hunting with Leonard Sears. The two men were hiding in separate clumps in the Chequesset Neck marsh when a duck came flying past. Both men fired. Henry missed and Lennie also missed the duck but not Henry who received part of a charge of birdshot in his rear leg. Fortunately, because of the distance, the shot only penetrated the skin. They were later removed by Dr. Bell but he is still limping. Was it worth it, Henry?

Mysterious lights seen flashing from the shore near the Nobscusset Inn have led to rumors that German spies may be communicating with a submarine in the Bay. Police Chief Nye says it is his opinion that the lights are the work of pranksters but, whichever it is, they will be in for a hot surprise if he catches them. That's the kind of talk we like to hear, Chief!

L'Envoi

AND SO the golden summer sped onward. At its beginning the days and weeks and even months seemed to stretch ahead to infinity, but there were portents of its passing.

As time went by, rambler roses gave way to gladiolus, and asters bloomed along the sandy road to Gull Pond. Corn ripened in Uncle Ben Eaton's garden and apples reddened on his gnarled orchard trees.

More time passed and we noticed that when we walked to the post office for the evening mail, it was dark by the time we returned to the cottage. After mid-August the nights took on a chill, making sweaters mandatory. There was even a different look to the ocean, a steelier blue that hinted of changes to come. Rafts of scoters—the gunner's coot—began to appear offshore. There were changes in the marshes, too, a faint yellowing of the sedge grass and a gathering of shorebirds, making ready for their southward migrations.

These signs of change were apparent for all to read, but so gradual was their approach that they went unheeded. And then, suddenly, seemingly out of nowhere, Labor Day was at hand! The discovery brought with it mingled gloom and anticipation. There was gloom at having these magic days of summer come to an end, but it was somewhat tempered by the anticipation of resuming our interrupted lives at home—our friends, our projects, our hobbies, even a return to the regimentation of school.

The pace quickened as Labor Day weekend approached. There was so much to be done and so little time left in which to do it. There was a final trip down the bay with Cap'n Dill and Cap'n Lambert, a last trip to the ponds for perch and pickerel, a farewell visit to Cahoon's Hollow and Highland Light, and perhaps one more trip to Province-town—each excursion poignant with the realization that there would be no more that year.

On Saturday Mr. Hopkins arrived on the noon train to close the cottage and to fetch his family home to Springfield. Sometimes the cottage closing was interrupted in favor of a quick expedition to Gull Pond, but there was a definite sense of finality when Mr. Hopkins appeared upon the scene.

Perishable or valuable—to Mr. Hopkins—items in the barn had to be moved into the house, swings and hammocks had to be taken down and stored, and storm doors and shutters made ready to protect the cottage from winter gales.

In our apartment, trunks that had long stood empty now gaped to receive their contents of sheets, pillowcases, towels and clothing. And on Saturday afternoon the expressman, Teeter-ass Newcomb, came to collect them and put them aboard the three o'clock train.

"By gawd, Doc, you must have a battleship anchor in this wardrobe trunk!"

Down at Holbrook's Livery Stable the Pope-Hartford was undergoing a thorough check-up for the long journey home.

"I hope that magneto ain't going to quit on you. By rights you'd ought to have a new one but I'd have to send to

Boston to get one. I've patched it up best I can and it'll probably hold together, as the feller says."

On Sunday Eddie Baker came to dismantle the pump and now things were really coming down to the wire. "Better have the boys pump all the water you'll need till you leave, Mis' Janes."

We always seemed to require an inordinate amount, and Cousin Alfred and I were kept busy filling tubs, buckets, pots and pans. When we had finished, Eddie hauled up length after length of pipe, took off the handle and wrapped the pump in layers of burlap.

Sunday was also the day when goodbyes had to be said, not only to people, but also to places—to the bay beach, the ocean, to Nye's Souvenir Shop, to the harbor and to Chequesset Inn and our friends among its guests. The Chequesset Inn closed the day after Labor Day and over the weekend the pier on which it stood was lined with the trunks of departing guests—a melancholy scene.

On Sunday evening the last meeting was held in Mr.
Hopkins's barn. The tales that were told, the quahaugs and
beer consumed that night in the lantern's yellow glow had
to last for the next ten months. Meanwhile, out on the front
porch, the Andover boy was strumming softly on his
ukulele and rendering "By the Light of the Silvery Moon."
Doris was close to tears.

Bedtime came early that evening, for we had to be up
with the dawn to finish packing suitcases, to clear out our
possessions cached behind pictures on the bedroom walls, to
give the floors a final sweeping, and to load the Pope-Hartford.

Then on to the Curran House and breakfast. An hour
later the inevitable moment was at hand and could not be
further postponed. Slowly we rolled through the deserted
village streets and turned into the King's Highway. On we
drove through South Wellfleet, Eastham, Orleans, Brewster, Dennis, Yarmouth, Barnstable, Sandwich—and now
the Bourne Bridge rose ahead. When we had crossed the
Canal, Cape Cod and summer lay behind us for another
year.

"Five and four-tenths miles. Turn left at fork by red barn
and join trolley tracks which follow all the way to
Wareham. . . ."

This is the Cape Cod I remember. Much of it has
disappeared forever, buried deep beneath superhighways,
real estate developments, shopping centers, new technolo-
gies and changing times. The old-time baymen are gone,
the life savers, the sea captains. Gone, too, are the sailing
vessels, the sandy roads, the two-wheeled blue carts and the
trains.

The Chequesset Inn prospered through the Twenties, but then the depression years, combined with the advent of tourist homes, faster transportation and a less leisurely type of vacationer who came for weekends rather than weeks caused the old landmark to fall upon evil days. The end came in 1934 when ice jams formed around the pilings and carried away the pier. Like some gallant ship, Chequesset Inn slid into the sea and by the next summer no trace of it was left.

And yet much remains today of the Cape Cod I remember. White sand beaches and the vast expanse of ocean, the surge and resurge of surf, sunrise and sunset, calm and storm, blue vistas glimpsed between the dunes, ponds shimmering in pine-grown hollows, weathered, shingled houses, bayberries and beach plums straggling across cranberry-carpeted moors, fresh breezes of salty air, gulls circling overhead—these continue unchanged and will endure until the sea at last reclaims the Narrow Land.